Advanced Introduction to Space La

Elgar Advanced Introductions are stimulating and thoughtful introductions to major fields in the social sciences and law, expertly written by the world's leading scholars. Designed to be accessible yet rigorous, they offer concise and lucid surveys of the substantive and policy issues associated with discrete subject areas.

The aims of the series are two-fold: to pinpoint essential principles of a particular field, and to offer insights that stimulate critical thinking. By distilling the vast and often technical corpus of information on the subject into a concise and meaningful form, the books serve as accessible introductions for undergraduate and graduate students coming to the subject for the first time. Importantly, they also develop well-informed, nuanced critiques of the field that will challenge and extend the understanding of advanced students, scholars and policy-makers.

For a full list of titles in the series please see the back of the book. Recent titles in the series include:

The Creative City
Charles Landry

Sustainable Tourism
David Weaver

International Trade Law
Michael J. Trebilcock and Joel Trachtman

Austrian School of Economics
Second Edition
Randall G. Holcombe

European Union Law
Jacques Ziller

U.S. Criminal Procedure
Christopher Slobogin

Feminist Economics
Joyce P. Jacobsen

Platform Economics
Robin Mansell and W. Edward Steinmueller

Planning Theory
Robert A. Beauregard

Public Finance
Vito Tanzi

Tourism Destination Management
Chris Ryan

Human Dignity and Law
James R. May and Erin Daly

International Investment Law
August Reinisch

Space Law
Frans G. von der Dunk

Advanced Introduction to
Space Law

FRANS G. VON DER DUNK

Associate Professor, Faculty of Law and Administration, Lazarski University, Warsaw, Poland, and Professor of Space Law, University of Nebraska College of Law, Lincoln, USA

Elgar Advanced Introductions

Cheltenham, UK • Northampton, MA, USA

© Frans G. von der Dunk 2020

All rights reserved. No part of this publication may be reproduced, stored in a retrieval system or transmitted in any form or by any means, electronic, mechanical or photocopying, recording, or otherwise without the prior permission of the publisher.

Published by
Edward Elgar Publishing Limited
The Lypiatts
15 Lansdown Road
Cheltenham
Glos GL50 2JA
UK

Edward Elgar Publishing, Inc.
William Pratt House
9 Dewey Court
Northampton
Massachusetts 01060
USA

A catalogue record for this book
is available from the British Library

Library of Congress Control Number: 2020942914

ISBN 978 1 78990 185 6 (cased)
ISBN 978 1 78990 187 0 (paperback)
ISBN 978 1 78990 186 3 (eBook)

Typeset by Servis Filmsetting Ltd, Stockport, Cheshire
Printed and bound by CPI Group (UK) Ltd, Croydon, CR0 4YY

Contents

List of figures vii
List of abbreviations viii

1 The concept of space law 1
  1.1 Outer space, space activities and the law 1
  1.2 The structure of 'space law' 3
  1.3 The legal value of the structural provisions of the Outer Space Treaty 6
  1.4 The substance of 'space law' 8
  1.5 The structure of this book 10

2 The inner core: space law *stricto sensu* 14
  2.1 Introduction 14
  2.2 The Outer Space Treaty 16
  2.3 The Rescue Agreement 25
  2.4 The Liability Convention 28
  2.5 The Registration Convention 33
  2.6 Space customary international law: the case of 'space debris' 37
  2.7 Concluding remarks 39

3 The 'Northern' part of the first ring of space law 42
  3.1 Introduction 42
  3.2 The Intergovernmental Agreement on the International Space Station 44
  3.3 The ITSO Agreement and the IMSO Convention 47
  3.4 The ESA Convention 51
  3.5 The Moon Agreement and space mining 54
  3.6 The UN Principles on Remote Sensing and customary international law 59
  3.7 Concluding remarks 64

4	The 'Southern' part of the first ring of space law	66
	4.1 Introduction	66
	4.2 The international regime on the international use of radio frequencies in space	67
	4.3 International law on military activities and operations in space	72
	4.4 The international regimes addressing sensitive dual-use space technologies	83
	4.5 Concluding remarks	89
5	The second ring of space law	92
	5.1 Introduction	92
	5.2 Intellectual property rights in the context of space activities	94
	5.3 Air law and private manned spaceflight, including space tourism	99
	5.4 The international trade regime for satellite communication services	108
	5.5 Concluding remarks	112
6	The third ring: national space legislation	115
	6.1 Introduction	115
	6.2 National space legislation addressing private sector space activities	117
	6.3 Scope and approach of national space legislation	121
	6.4 Concluding remarks	124
7	The future of space law	126

Bibliography	128
Index	137

Figures

1.1	The schematic conceptual structure of space law *largo sensu*	11
2.1	The inner core: space law *stricto sensu*	17
3.1	The 'Northern' part of the first ring of space law	43
4.1	The 'Southern' part of the first ring of space law	67
5.1	The second ring of space law	93
6.1	The third ring: national space legislation	117

Abbreviations

ABM	anti-ballistic missile
AECA	Arms Export Control Act
ASAT	anti-satellite weapons
BSS	broadcasting-satellite services
CCL	Commerce Control List
CGEA	Community General Export Authorization
CNES	*Centre National d'Etudes Spatiales*
CONAE	National Commission on Space Activities
COPUOS	Committee on the Peaceful Uses of Outer Space
EAA	Export Administration Act
EARs	Export Administration Regulations
EASA	European Aviation Safety Agency
EEC	European Economic Community
ENMOD	Environmental Modification
ESA	European Space Agency
EU	European Union
EUTELSAT	European Telecommunications Satellite Organization
FSS	fixed-satellite services
GATS	General Agreement on Trade in Services
GIS	Geographic Information Systems
GMDSS	Global Maritime Distress and Safety System
IADC	Inter-Agency Space Debris Consultation Committee
ICAO	International Civil Aviation Organization
ICOC	International Code of Conduct against Ballistic Missile Proliferation
IGOs	intergovernmental organizations
IMSO	International Mobile Satellite Organization
INMARSAT	International Mobile Satellite Organization
INTELSAT	International Telecommunications Satellite Organization
ISS	International Space Station
ITARs	International Traffic in Arms Regulations

ITSO	International Telecommunications Satellite Organization
ITU	International Telecommunication Union
MFN	Most-Favoured Nation
MSS	mobile-satellite services
MTCR	Missile Technology Control Regime
NASA	National Aeronautics and Space Administration
NT	National Treatment
OCST	Office for Commercial Space Transportation
PPWT	Draft Treaty on the Prevention of the Placement of Weapons in Outer Space, the Threat or Use of Force against Outer Space Objects
PSOs	Protected Space Operations
PTOs	public telecommunication operators
RLVs	reusable launch vehicles
SARPs	Standards and Recommended Practices
SDI	Strategic Defense Initiative
TT&C	telemetry, tracking & control
UN	United Nations
UNIDROIT	International Institute for the Unification of Private Law
UNOOSA	UN Office of Outer Space Affairs
US	United States
USML	US Munitions List
WARC	World Administrative Radio Conference
WIPO	World Intellectual Property Organization
WRC	World Radio Conference
WTO	World Trade Organization

1 The concept of space law

1.1 Outer space, space activities and the law

'Wherever You Go, the Taxman Goes' ran a 2009 headline in the *New York Times*, alluding to the seemingly inescapable ubiquity of that infamous phenomenon of the tax collector.[1] This neat one-liner is a good point of departure for the analysis of 'space law' as well: 'wherever humans go, the law follows', and this is also true in outer space. Only once humankind entered the realm of outer space did the legal aspects of such endeavours start to occupy the minds of more than just a few visionaries and legal theoreticians. The shortest way of defining 'space law' therefore would be 'all law that actually, one way or another, follows humans into outer space'.

Thereby, it addresses in principle an unlimited array of human activities, interactions and interests which, throughout history, on Earth have often already been dealt with by way of myriad different legal regimes without usually taking the special 'space-characteristics' into consideration. In other words, space law would be 'every legal or regulatory regime having a significant impact, even if implicitly or indirectly, on at least one type of space activity or major space application',[2] regardless of whether such a regime has taken the specifics of application to outer space or space activities into account.

On closer look, however, the issue is a bit more complicated.

Outer space is often viewed as the fourth geographical realm for human activity, following the territories, the seas and the airspaces

---

[1] D.L. Jacobs, Wherever You Go, the Taxman Goes, *New York Times*, 1 April 2009, https://www.nytimes.com/2009/04/02/business/retirementspecial/02relocate.html (last accessed 16 June 2020).
[2] F.G. von der Dunk, Preface, in *Handbook of Space Law* (Eds. F.G. von der Dunk & F. Tronchetti) (2015), xxvi.

respectively, yet it is ultimately different in character.[3] To start with, contrary to the other three realms, outer space is conceived as fundamentally being 'without frontiers' (with the exception of a – so far undefined – 'lower boundary' separating it from airspaces). More notably and importantly, 'man' usually 'goes' into that realm of outer space by proxy.

Law indeed generally addresses persons (or legal entities created by them and somehow representing them, whether this concerns States, private companies or other legal concepts) and then deals with the activities they undertake wherever they are, whether on the ground, on the seas or in the air. This means that the subjects of the law and the activities conducted by them, which trigger consequences pursuant to such law, happen to be in the same general location. In contrast, space law has to deal with the reality that most human-driven activities in outer space are, in fact, conducted from Earth.

Of course, humans actually ventured into outer space, and those activities have captured the awe and imagination much more than mundane space activities such as those conducted using satellites. However, in terms of size, scope and impact, more formidable than what these few humans have ever been able to achieve in outer space is what has resulted from operations of radio-controlled spacecraft guided from Earth, by humans pulling handles and pushing buttons somewhere in a terrestrial control station. In other words, the persons subject to any rules, rights and obligations pursuant to applicable law are not anywhere near to where the consequences of their acts play out at least in first instance.

Consequently, the classical, neat division of the legal world into areas subject to territorial jurisdiction – where the laws of one or the other sovereign State with few exceptions rule supreme – plus a few areas outside any particular State's territorial jurisdiction – where the laws of many States, as based on the nationality of the persons or entities involved, can interact subject to some public international law regime generally recognized, even adhered to by those States – does not work that neatly anymore in outer space.

---

3 See further on this *e.g.* F.G. von der Dunk, Surveying the Scene: The Effects of Globalisation on Space Law – A Panellist's Remarks, in *Globalisation – The State and International Law* (Ed. S. Hobe) (2009), 128–9.

1.2 The structure of 'space law'

The most fundamental cluster of rules of 'space law' as enshrined in the Outer Space Treaty,[4] in turn the most fundamental treaty addressing humankind's ventures into outer space, concerns the determination that there is such a realm as 'outer space', somehow geographically bounded,[5] where the same territorial sovereignty that is so common to our terrestrial legal systems does not extend and freedom of activity, at least for States, is the default regime. Such freedom is then only (to be) bounded and conditioned by applicable rules of public international law, read international treaties and customary international law as binding upon particular sets of States.[6]

More precisely, '[o]uter space, including the Moon and other celestial bodies, is not subject to national appropriation by claim of sovereignty, by means of use or occupation, or by any other means'.[7] Following this clause, the 'exploration and use of outer space' is endowed with the status of 'the province of all mankind', resulting in a legal status for outer space as such best likened to a kind of global commons, giving rise to the freedom of 'exploration and use by all States', including the 'freedom of scientific investigation'.[8]

In such respects, outer space is most commonly legally equated with the area of the high seas, where also the freedom to act provides the

---

4 Treaty on Principles Governing the Activities of States in the Exploration and Use of Outer Space, including the Moon and Other Celestial Bodies (hereafter Outer Space Treaty), London/Moscow/Washington, done 27 January 1967, entered into force 10 October 1967; 610 UNTS 205; TIAS 6347; 18 UST 2410; UKTS 1968 No. 10; Cmnd. 3198; ATS 1967 No. 24; 6 ILM 386 (1967).
5 See further *infra*, § 5.3, esp. at n. 371, for a brief discussion of the boundary issue.
6 See Art. 38(1) (a) and (b), Statute of the International Court of Justice (San Francisco, done 26 June 1945, entered into force 24 October 1945; 156 UNTS 77; USTS 993; 59 Stat. 1031; UKTS 1946 No. 67; ATS 1945 No. 1); generally recognized as representing the two major sources of public international law; see further *e.g.* A. Cassese, *International Law* (2001), 119 ff.; G. Boas, *Public International Law* (2012), 52 ff.
7 Art. II, Outer Space Treaty (*supra* n. 4). See further F.G. von der Dunk, *Private Enterprise and Public Interest in the European 'Spacescape'* (1997), 12–17; S.R. Freeland & R.S. Jakhu, Article II, in *Cologne Commentary on Space Law* (Eds. S. Hobe, B. Schmidt-Tedd & K.U. Schrogl) *Vol. I* (2009), 44–63; S.U. Reif, B. Schmidt-Tedd & K. Wannenmacher, Report of the 'Project 2001' Working Group on Privatisation, in *'Project 2001' – Legal Framework for the Commercial Use of Outer Space* (Ed. K.H. Böckstiegel) (2002), 429–33.
8 Art. I, Outer Space Treaty (*supra* n. 4). See further S. Hobe, Article I, in *Cologne Commentary on Space Law* (Eds. S. Hobe, B. Schmidt-Tedd & K.U. Schrogl) *Vol. I* (2009), 25–43.

baseline legal regime, as expressed by the famous *dictum* in the Lotus case:

> International law governs relations between independent States. The rules of law binding upon States therefore emanate from their own free will as expressed in conventions or by usages generally accepted as expressing principles of law and established in order to regulate the relations between these co-existing independent communities or with a view to the achievement of common aims. Restrictions upon the independence of States therefore cannot be presumed.[9]

It is then up to individual States to determine whether and to what extent they would allow non-State entities under their jurisdiction to benefit from this baseline freedom as well, noting that importantly those States *themselves* will directly be held responsible for such activities of relevant non-State entities:

> States Parties to the Treaty shall bear international responsibility for national activities in outer space, including the Moon and other celestial bodies, whether such activities are carried on by governmental agencies or by non-governmental entities, and for assuring that national activities are carried out in conformity with the provisions set forth in the present Treaty. The activities of non-governmental entities in outer space, including the Moon and other celestial bodies, shall require authorization and continuing supervision by the appropriate State Party to the Treaty.[10]

While this Article only refers to obligations contained 'in the present Treaty', given the fundamental character and importance of the Outer Space Treaty, this has come to refer to any obligation under international space law, as essentially an elaboration of the former.[11] This is further corroborated by Article III, which principally imports all of

---

9 SS Lotus (Fr./Turk.) 1927 PCIJ Rep. (ser. A) No. 10, at 44; see also Art. 87, United Nations Convention on the Law of the Sea, Montego Bay, done 10 December 1982, entered into force 16 November 1994; 1833 UNTS 3 & 1835 UNTS 261; UKTS 1999 No. 81; Cmnd. 8941; ATS 1994 No. 31; 21 ILM 1261 (1982); S. Treaty Doc. No. 103–39.

10 Art. VI, Outer Space Treaty (*supra* n. 4). See Von der Dunk, *supra* n. 7, 17–22; M. Gerhard, Art. VI, in *Cologne Commentary on Space Law* (Eds. S. Hobe, B. Schmidt-Tedd & K.U. Schrogl) *Vol. I* (2009), 103–25; Reif, Schmidt-Tedd & Wannenmacher, *supra* n. 7, 411–23.

11 See further B. Cheng, *Studies in International Space Law* (1997), 215–64; F. Lyall & P.B. Larsen, *Space Law – A Treatise* (2009), 53–80; M. Lachs, *The Law of Outer Space* (reprint 2010), 11–64; P. Malanczuk, Space Law as a Branch of International Law, 25 *Netherlands International Law Yearbook* (1994), 143–80.

general international law into the Outer Space Treaty and thereby into space law (at least as long as it is not superseded, read contradicted, by the *lex specialis* of space law).[12]

In particular the last phrase of Article VI quoted above has by now given rise *inter alia* to more than two dozen States having adopted national space legislation to ensure that such private space activities would be compliant with whatever legal limits international space law imposes upon these activities.[13] As complementary to the State's responsibility for private space activities, such national space laws have also dealt with the State's liability for international damage, including if caused by such private space activities, equally following from the Outer Space Treaty:

> Each State Party to the Treaty that launches or procures the launching of an object into outer space, including the Moon and other celestial bodies, and each State Party from whose territory or facility an object is launched, is internationally liable for damage to another State Party to the Treaty or to its natural or juridical persons by such object or its component parts on the Earth, in air space or in outer space.[14]

This Article has been interpreted, clarified and elaborated by the 1972 Liability Convention,[15] which further underpinned the State-focused nature of third-party liability for damage caused by space activities in the international realm.

A further essential element of the construct of international space law is the provision establishing some form of quasi-territorial jurisdiction over registered space objects and 'personnel thereof', where Article VIII of the Outer Space Treaty provides States, in the absence of true territorially based jurisdictional competences in outer space, with another, more focused and limited legal tool to control relevant private

---

12 See further *infra*, § 2.2.
13 See further *infra*, Chapter 6.
14 Art. VII, Outer Space Treaty (*supra* n. 4). See further Von der Dunk, *supra* n. 7, 22–6; A. Kerrest de Rozavel & L.J. Smith, Article VII, in *Cologne Commentary on Space Law* (Eds. S. Hobe, B. Schmidt-Tedd & K.U. Schrogl) *Vol. I* (2009), 126–45; Reif, Schmidt-Tedd & Wannenmacher, *supra* n. 7, 411, 423–8.
15 Convention on International Liability for Damage Caused by Space Objects (hereafter Liability Convention), London/Moscow/Washington, done 29 March 1972, entered into force 1 September 1972; 961 UNTS 187; TIAS 7762; 24 UST 2389; UKTS 1974 No. 16; Cmnd. 5068; ATS 1975 No. 5; 10 ILM 965 (1971). See further *infra*, § 2.4.

activities in space.[16] This Article has in turn been further elaborated by means of the 1975 Registration Convention.[17]

These few Articles can be said to jointly structure, in a fundamental manner, the legal status of outer space and the law applicable to that area that comes with it, by essentially determining in what cases, scenarios and events, and subject to which parameters, States can also be held accountable as to how they would go about taking care of such accountability – without (as of yet) going into specific substantive details of what is obligatory, allowable or prohibited in terms of outer space and space activities.

1.3 The legal value of the structural provisions of the Outer Space Treaty

The above nature and structure of space law also raises the issue of the precise legal value of these principles and rules. While the Outer Space Treaty carries the ratifications of 110 States plus the signatures of 23 more,[18] this still leaves some 90 countries not being parties to the Treaty and some 70, technically speaking, not even under an obligation 'to refrain from acts which would defeat the object and purpose of a treaty'.[19]

Yet it has generally come to be accepted that – in deviation from the standard approach to treaty law as per the 'Lotus principle'[20] – the

---

16 Art. VIII, Outer Space Treaty (*supra* n. 4), provides in relevant part: 'A State Party to the Treaty on whose registry an object launched into outer space is carried shall retain jurisdiction and control over such object, and over any personnel thereof, while in outer space or on a celestial body'. See further Von der Dunk, *supra* n. 7, 27–32; B. Schmidt-Tedd & S. Mick, Article VIII, in *Cologne Commentary on Space Law* (Eds. S. Hobe, B. Schmidt-Tedd & K.U. Schrogl) *Vol. I* (2009), 146–68; Reif, Schmidt-Tedd & Wannenmacher, *supra* n. 7, 428–9.
17 Convention on Registration of Objects Launched into Outer Space (hereafter Registration Convention), New York, done 14 January 1975, entered into force 15 September 1976; 1023 UNTS 15; TIAS 8480; 28 UST 695; UKTS 1978 No. 70; Cmnd. 6256; ATS 1986 No. 5; 14 ILM 43 (1975). See further *infra*, § 2.5.
18 As of 1 January 2020; see https://www.unoosa.org/documents/pdf/spacelaw/treatystatus/TreatiesStatus-2020E.pdf (last accessed 16 June 2020).
19 Art. 18, Vienna Convention on the Law of Treaties, Vienna, done 23 May 1969, entered into force 27 January 1980; 1155 UNTS 331; UKTS 1980 No. 58; Cmnd. 4818; ATS 1974 No. 2; 8 ILM 679 (1969); providing in this context that 'A State is obliged to refrain from acts which would defeat the object and purpose of a treaty when: (a) it has signed the treaty or has exchanged instruments constituting the treaty subject to ratification, acceptance or approval, until it shall have made its intention clear not to become a party to the treaty'.
20 See *supra*, (text at) n. 9.

Outer Space Treaty, certainly as to the structural aspects discussed above, would also bind those States not having ratified or signed it, at long as no major valid arguments can be discerned to the contrary.

To begin with, these structural aspects fundamentally determining the legal status of a realm are a matter of 'all-or-nothing', elevating the legal impact of the relevant clauses to that of a law-making treaty providing clauses of an *erga omnes* character comprising an 'objective regime'.[21] If one State ignored the status of outer space and its exploration and use as a 'province of all mankind' or denied responsibility and liability for relevant space activities, the whole legal structure would quickly and inevitably come crashing down, essentially giving rise to a lawless legal vacuum to the detriment of all humankind and all States. For such reasons, the Treaty has often been labelled (rather loosely) the 'Magna Carta' for (outer) space,[22] or (much more accurately) as 'containing several key provisions of "constitutional" significance'.[23]

Further to this, the Treaty's parties encompass basically all spacefaring nations, whereas the States not included by and large concern small, poor States that have so far shown little interest and less capability in becoming active in outer space. As the International Court of Justice has made clear, 'States whose interests are specially affected'[24] play a particularly important role in the determination of whether something qualifies as a rule of customary international law. If the former set of States have agreed on the legal status of outer space and the resulting general structure of space law, it would not be for any of the others to

---

21 See further J. Crawford, *Brownlie's Principles of Public International Law* (8th ed.) (2012), 31–2, 348; C. Fernández de Casadevante Romani, Objective Regime, in *The Max Planck Encyclopedia of Public International Law* (Ed. R. Wolfrum) Vol. VII (2012), 912–15; also J.A. Frowein, Obligations *erga omnes*, in *The Max Planck Encyclopedia of Public International Law* (Ed. R. Wolfrum) Vol. VII (2012), 916–20; specifically on the Outer Space Treaty in such a context G. Lafferranderie, Introduction, in *Outlook on Space Law over the Next 30 Years* (Eds. G. Lafferranderie & D. Crowther) (1997), 1–6; V.S. Vereshchetin & G.M. Danilenko, Custom as a Source of International Law of Outer Space, 13 *Journal of Space Law* (1985), 22–35; A. Soucek, International Law, in *Outer Space in Society, Politics and Law* (Eds. C. Brünner & A. Soucek) (2011), 299–332.
22 As coined for the first time by William Hyman as the title for his book on the, at that time still nascent, Outer Space Treaty (*supra* n. 4); W.A. Hyman, *Magna Carta of Space* (1966).
23 D.A. Koplow, Exoatmospheric Plowshares: Using a Nuclear Explosive Device for Planetary Defense Against an Incoming Asteroid, 23 *UCLA Journal of International Law and Foreign Affairs* (2019), 105; further referencing Lyall & Larsen, *supra* n. 11, 49–73; P.G. Dembling & D.M. Arons, The Evolution of the Outer Space Treaty, 33 *Journal of Air Law & Commerce* (1967), 419.
24 North Sea Continental Shelf Cases (Ger./Den.; Ger./Neth.) 1969 ICJ Rep. 3 (Feb. 20), at 74.

ignore those, once they *did* start to show substantial interest and/or capabilities with regard to outer space.

Here, the case of the 1959 Antarctic Treaty[25] is highly illustrative. The 12 countries at the time deploying (largely scientific) activities on the continent purported to determine the general legal status of a geographical area (in this case of course Antarctica) and thereby also fundamentally determine the application to that realm of international law as well as of national laws of States concerned. When, over the course of time, other countries wanted to become and/or actually became active in Antarctica, rather than devising their own take on its legal status, they undertook efforts to become accepted as 'Consultative Parties' to the Antarctic Treaty, the status allowing them to participate in all the decision-making related to new laws and treaties applicable to the area within the parameters of the Antarctic Treaty and follow-on treaties in force with respect to that area.[26]

1.4 The substance of 'space law'

It is within the structural provisions of the Outer Space Treaty discussed above that any relevant substantive rules, rights and obligations, basically regardless of their specific sources, will be found to operate. This substance of space law for the sake of convenience should be seen furthermore as deriving from a number of essentially overlapping legal regimes, in view of the global commons character of outer space, each of them firstly at an international level and secondly at a national level.

The overarching, still foundational legal regime is that of international space law *stricto sensu*, the *corpus iuris spatialis internationalis*, conceptually speaking the inner 'core' of international space law applicable to basically all space activities as well as very much exclusively focused thereon. Occasionally this also includes rules pertinent to downstream applications of space activities, the standard assumption being that

---

25 Antarctic Treaty, Washington, done 1 December 1959, entered into force 23 June 1961; 402 UNTS 71; TIAS 4780; 12 UST 794; UKTS 1961 No. 97; Cmnd. 913; ATS 1961 No. 12.
26 See Arts. IX, X, XII, esp. XIII, Antarctic Treaty (*supra* n. 25); further *e.g.* S. Vöneky & S. Addison-Agyei, Antarctica, in *The Max Planck Encyclopedia of Public International Law* (Ed. R. Wolfrum) *Vol. I* (2012), 420 ff., esp. 433–4.

space activities in one way or another should benefit people, societies and States on Earth.[27]

Around that inner core a first conceptual 'ring' of space law concerns sets of international rules either not applicable to all space activities yet focused very much on what space activities it *does* apply to, or conversely, applicable to basically all space activities but not focused on space activities *alone*. Both would as a default bow to the specifics of the core, as – from a space perspective at least – constituting *lex generalis* compared with the *lex specialis* of the core.[28]

Beyond that, a second conceptual 'ring' consists of international law which is relevant for some space activities even while not specifically focusing on them, yet which because of their important effects on 'at least one type of space activity or major space application'[29] should be considered part of space law *largo sensu*. Here, again as a default the law in this ring would essentially bow to the specifics of the core *and* the first ring as constituting the *lex specialis* compared with the *lex generalis* of the second ring.

A final, outer conceptual 'ring' concerns national space legislation. Among others, it implements, applies and/or interprets the rules of the core and (usually at least to some extent) the inner two rings domestically, and in any event has to operate within the limitations provided by the legal status of outer space and the structure of international space law as set out above.

All such distinctions should, of course, not obscure the main fact that, as the definition provided earlier indicates, 'space law' ultimately presents a conglomerate of legal regimes, international as well as national, which were developed in different contexts and from various angles.

For example, a communications satellite operator, in order to ensure the legitimacy of its operations, needs to comply both with space law *stricto sensu* (such as the Outer Space Treaty or Liability Convention

---

27 *Cf.* also Art. I, Outer Space Treaty (*supra* n. 4).
28 This ties in with the general interpretation of the impact of Art. III, Outer Space Treaty (*supra* n. 4) as briefly discussed *supra* at § 1.2. See on the concepts of *lex specialis*, *lex generalis* and the relationship between the two *e.g.* H. Thirlway, The Sources of International Law, in *International Law* (Ed. M.D. Evans) (2003), 136–41; M.A. Shaw, *International Law* (4th ed.) (1997), 96; Crawford, *supra* n. 21, 22.
29 Von der Dunk, *supra* n. 2, xxvi.

already referred to), with telecommunications law (to the extent satellites are not explicitly or logically excluded), with intellectual property rights law (patents, for instance), and with international trade law (to provide rights of access to commercial service markets) – to name just the most important ones.

Correspondingly, if States, either on their own domestically or jointly on the international level, were looking to promote by legal means satellite communications while curbing the perceived potential risks and drawbacks, they would have to address the complete picture, that is, this same conglomerate of legal regimes. Both, moreover, domestically as much as internationally.

Noting furthermore that in the real world the dividing lines between law which *does* and law which *does not* at least predominantly address outer space and space activities are often not that clear-cut and/or drawn in a somewhat subjective manner, Figure 1.1 merely represents a schematic conceptual picture of space law *largo sensu*, which is then nevertheless followed as a means of organizing the multi-faceted contents of space law – and hence of this book.

1.5 The structure of this book

Following the schematic approach outlined above, Chapter 2 will firstly address the main elements of the core, essentially comprising the aforementioned Outer Space Treaty, the Liability Convention and the Registration Convention, as well as the 1968 Rescue Agreement[30] and one particularly important area of customary international law development bearing some relationship to those treaties, namely that of space debris.

Chapter 3 will then address the most important elements of the 'Northern' part of the first ring, comprising the 1979 Moon Agreement[31] as well as a few premier examples of treaties underpin-

---

30 Agreement on the Rescue of Astronauts, the Return of Astronauts and the Return of Objects Launched into Outer Space (hereafter Rescue Agreement), London/Moscow/Washington, done 22 April 1968, entered into force 3 December 1968; 672 UNTS 119; TIAS 6599; 19 UST 7570; UKTS 1969 No. 56; Cmnd. 3786; ATS 1986 No. 8; 7 ILM 151 (1968).

31 Agreement Governing the Activities of States on the Moon and Other Celestial Bodies (hereafter Moon Agreement), New York, done 18 December 1979, entered into force 11 July 1984; 1363 UNTS 3; ATS 1986 No. 14; 18 ILM 1434 (1979).

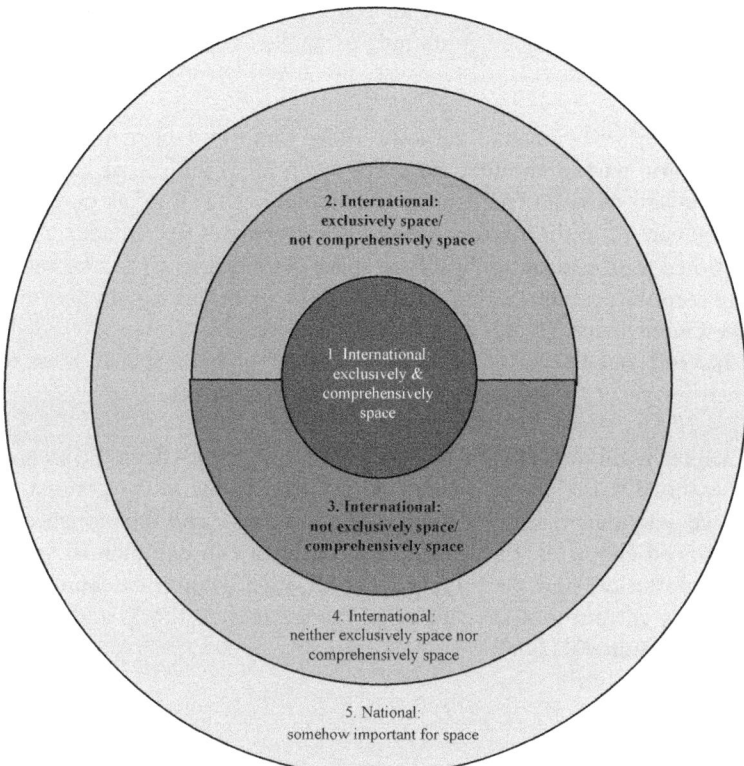

Figure 1.1 The schematic conceptual structure of space law *largo sensu*

ning specific collaboration efforts: the Intergovernmental Agreement on the ISS,[32] the ITSO Agreement,[33] the IMSO Convention[34] and the

---

[32] Agreement among the Government of Canada, Governments of Member States of the European Space Agency, the Government of Japan, the Government of the Russian Federation, and the Government of the United States of America concerning Cooperation on the Civil International Space Station (hereafter Intergovernmental Agreement on the ISS), Washington, done 29 January 1998, entered into force 27 March 2001; TIAS 12927; Cm. 4552; *Space Law – Basic Legal Documents*, D.II.4.

[33] Agreement Relating to the International Telecommunications Satellite Organization (ITSO) (hereafter ITSO Agreement), Washington, done 20 August 1971, entered into force 12 February 1973, as amended 13 November 2000, amended version entered into force 30 November 2004; Cm. 5092; *Space Law – Basic Legal Documents*, C.V.1.

[34] Convention on the International Mobile Satellite Organization (hereafter IMSO Convention), London, done 3 September 1976, entered into force 16 July 1979, as amended 1998, amended version entered into force 31 July 2001; ATS 2001 No. 11.

ESA Convention.[35] In addition, an example of the development of customary international law pertaining to satellite remote sensing will be briefly addressed.

Chapter 4 will continue with the most important elements of the 'Southern' part of the first ring. The main areas addressed here will be the use of radio frequencies and orbits/orbital slots as currently taken care of in the context of the ITU[36] as part of the broader international legal regime applicable to space activities, in particular satellite communications; military uses of outer space, principally (beyond the Outer Space Treaty) as per such more general treaties as the UN Charter[37] and the Partial Test Ban Treaty;[38] and the special issue of dual-use security-sensitive technology export controls.

Chapter 5 will then address a few illustrative examples from the second ring, notably the use of intellectual property rights in the context of space activities in view of their highly expensive and technologically advanced character; the involvement of air law in commercial space transportation; and the trade aspects of satellite communication services as currently taken care of in the context of the World Trade Organization (WTO).[39]

---

35 Convention for the Establishment of a European Space Agency (hereafter ESA Convention), Paris, done 30 May 1975, entered into force 30 October 1980; 1297 UNTS 161; UKTS 1981 No. 30; Cmnd. 8200; 14 ILM 864 (1975); *Space Law – Basic Legal Documents*, C.I.1.
36 The ITU is currently ruled by the Constitution of the International Telecommunication Union (hereafter ITU Constitution), Geneva, done 22 December 1992, entered into force 1 July 1994; 1825 UNTS 1; UKTS 1996 No. 24; Cm. 2539; ATS 1994 No. 28; Final Acts of the Additional Plenipotentiary Conference, Geneva, 1992 (1993), at 1; and the Convention of the International Telecommunication Union (hereafter ITU Convention), Geneva, done 22 December 1992, entered into force 1 July 1994; 1825 UNTS 1; UKTS 1996 No. 24; Cm. 2539; ATS 1994 No. 28; Final Acts of the Additional Plenipotentiary Conference, Geneva, 1992 (1993), at 71; both as amended a few times since; for the most recent versions of 2018, see http://search.itu.int/history/HistoryDigitalCollectionDocLibrary/5.22.61.en.100.pdf (last accessed 16 June 2020).
37 Charter of the United Nations (hereafter UN Charter), San Francisco, done 26 June 1945, entered into force 24 October 1945; USTS 993; 24 UST 2225; 59 Stat. 1031; 145 UKTS 805; UKTS 1946 No. 67; Cmd. 6666 & 6711; CTS 1945 No. 7; ATS 1945 No. 1.
38 Treaty Banning Nuclear Weapon Tests in the Atmosphere, in Outer Space and Under Water (hereafter Partial Test Ban Treaty), Moscow, done 5 August 1963, entered into force 10 October 1963; 480 UNTS 43; TIAS 5433; 14 UST 1313; UKTS 1964 No. 3; ATS 1963 No. 26.
39 The WTO was established by means of the Agreement Establishing the World Trade Organization (hereafter WTO Agreement), Marrakesh, done 15 April 1994, entered into force 1 January 1995; 1867 UNTS 154; UKTS 1996 No. 57; ATS 1995 No. 8; 33 ILM 1125, 1144 (1994).

Figure 1.1, of course, also refers to a third conceptual ring, of national space legislation. National space legislation, however, already as of today comes in so many different shapes, sizes and forms, certainly if it includes not only domestic law and regulation addressing exclusively and comprehensively space (essentially the national equivalent of the core of the *corpus iuris spatialis internationalis*) but also such law and regulation addressing only parts of the space sector (the equivalent of the Northern part of the first ring), addressing more than the space sector alone (the equivalent of the Southern part of the first ring) or addressing only part of the space sector as part of a much wider realm (the equivalent of the second ring). For that reason already, any comprehensive effort to analyse and summarize it goes beyond the present context, and Chapter 6 will therefore limit itself to making a few high-level abstract and generally cross-cutting observations on the topic, rather than provide for any substantive analyses or summaries.

Chapter 7 finally will provide some overarching concluding remarks, in particular regarding where space law may be headed in the foreseeable future and how such developments may best be guided.

2 The inner core: space law *stricto sensu*

2.1 Introduction

The core of the *corpus iuris spatialis internationalis* is generally viewed as consisting of five treaties drafted in the bosom of the United Nations, notably its Committee on the Peaceful Uses of Outer Space (COPUOS), and eight key UN General Assembly Resolutions.

Strictly speaking however, it is actually the Outer Space Treaty,[40] the Rescue Agreement,[41] the Liability Convention[42] and the Registration Convention[43] which provide the real inner core from our perspective as reflected by Figure 2.1: they are not only covering more or less all space activities imaginable, but are also widely ratified[44] and, in most cases and respects, considered to constitute customary international law.[45]

---

40 *Supra* n. 4.
41 *Supra* n. 30.
42 *Supra* n. 15.
43 *Supra* n. 17.
44 As of January 2020, the Outer Space Treaty (*supra* n. 4), counts 110 States parties and 23 more States as signatories; as for the Rescue Agreement (*supra* n. 30) these numbers are 98 and 23, respectively, for the Liability Convention (*supra* n. 15) they are 98 and 19, respectively, and for the Registration Convention (*supra* n. 17) they are 69 and 3, respectively. In each case, these include more or less all States relevant from the perspective of that particular treaty; see further https://www.unoosa.org/documents/pdf/spacelaw/treatystatus/TreatiesStatus-2020E.pdf (last accessed 16 June 2020).
45 As for the Outer Space Treaty (*supra* n. 4), see *supra* § 1.2. As for the other three treaties, they are essentially elaborations of specific clauses of the Outer Space Treaty; note that pursuant to the law of treaties the interpretation of clauses in the Outer Space Treaty should take into account '(a) any subsequent agreement between the parties regarding the interpretation of the treaty or the application of its provisions; [and] (b) any subsequent practice in the application of the treaty which establishes the agreement of the parties regarding its interpretation'; Art. 31(3), Vienna Convention on the Law of Treaties (*supra* n. 19). This effectively transforms those interpretations by the three follow-up treaties into something akin to customary international law. See in this respect for the Rescue Agreement (*supra* n. 30) *infra*, § 2.3 and Preamble, Art. 6, Rescue Agreement; also I. Marboe, J. Neumann & K.U. Schrogl, The 1968 Agreement on the Rescue of Astronauts, the Return of Astronauts and the Return of Objects Launched into Outer Space,

THE INNER CORE: SPACE LAW *STRICTO SENSU* 15

In contrast, the Moon Agreement,[46] the fifth UN space treaty to enter into force, is both ratified marginally (and by that token hardly of global legal impact), and focused on one set of space activities only, namely those pertaining to the Moon and other celestial bodies, as opposed to all activities taking place anywhere in the void of outer space.

As for the UN Resolutions, they are not legally binding as such, although they have been the subject of extended discussions regarding their potential value as representing, in whole or in part, customary international law. Three of those Resolutions – the 1982 Principles on Direct Broadcasting by Satellite,[47] the 1986 Principles on Remote Sensing[48] and the 1992 Principles on Nuclear Power Sources[49] – are focused on limited areas of space activity, as indicated by their titles, so they belong to the Northern part of the first ring in Figure 1.1.

Whereas the latter is not true of the 1963 Declaration on Principles,[50] its substance was meanwhile essentially incorporated into and thereby superseded by the Outer Space Treaty a few years later, and thus it

---

in *Cologne Commentary on Space Law* (Eds. S. Hobe, B. Schmidt-Tedd & K.U. Schrogl) *Vol. II* (2013), esp. 9–11, 21–2, 32–7; for the Liability Convention (*supra* n. 15) *infra*, § 2.4 and Preamble, Art. XXII(1), Liability Convention; also L.J. Smith, A. Kerrest de Rozavel & F. Tronchetti, The 1972 Convention on International Liability for Damage Caused by Space Objects, in *Cologne Commentary on Space Law* (Eds. S. Hobe, B. Schmidt-Tedd & K.U. Schrogl) *Vol. II* (2013), esp. 94–8, 100–2; for the Registration Convention (*supra* n. 17) *infra*, § 2.5 and Preamble, Art. VII(1), Registration Convention; also B. Schmidt-Tedd *et al.*, The 1975 Convention on Registration of Objects Launched into Outer Space, in *Cologne Commentary on Space Law* (Eds. S. Hobe, B. Schmidt-Tedd & K.U. Schrogl) *Vol. II* (2013), esp. 236–7, 239, 241–3.

46 *Supra* n. 31. See also further *infra*, § 3.5.
47 Principles Governing the Use by States of Artificial Earth Satellites for International Direct Television Broadcasting (hereafter Principles on Direct Broadcasting by Satellite), UNGA Res. 37/92, of 10 December 1982; UN Doc. A/AC.105/572/Rev.1, at 39. See further P. Stubbe, M. Ferrazzani & O. Huth, The 1982 Principles Governing the Use by States of Artificial Earth Satellites for International Direct Television Broadcasting, in *Cologne Commentary on Space Law* (Eds. S. Hobe, B. Schmidt-Tedd & K.U. Schrogl) *Vol. III* (2015), 1–79.
48 Principles Relating to Remote Sensing of the Earth from Outer Space (hereafter Principles on Remote Sensing), UNGA Res. 41/65, of 3 December 1986; UN Doc. A/AC.105/572/Rev.1, at 43; 25 ILM 1334 (1986). See further *infra*, § 3.6.
49 Principles Relevant to the Use of Nuclear Power Sources in Outer Space (hereafter Principles on Nuclear Power Sources), UNGA Res. 47/68, of 14 December 1992; UN Doc. A/AC.105/572/Rev.1, at 47. See further G.M. Goh *et al.*, The 1992 Principles Relevant to the Use of Nuclear Power Sources in Outer Space, in *Cologne Commentary on Space Law* (Eds. S. Hobe, B. Schmidt-Tedd & K.U. Schrogl) *Vol. III* (2015), 189–297.
50 Declaration of Legal Principles Governing the Activities of States in the Exploration and Use of Outer Space, UNGA Res. 1962(XVIII), of 13 December 1963; UN Doc. A/AC.105/572/Rev. 1, at 37.

does not merit separate treatment here. Conversely, three more recent Resolutions – the 1996 Benefits Declaration,[51] the 2004 Launching State Resolution[52] and the 2007 Registration Practice Resolution[53] – essentially provided for some harmonized and commonly agreed interpretation of, respectively, Article I of the Outer Space Treaty, the Liability Convention and the Registration Convention, wherefore they do not merit a separate discussion either. The most recent Resolution, the 2013 National Space Legislation Resolution,[54] will, as this already follows from its title, be addressed in the context of discussing the general role of national space legislation as per Chapter 6, which will also briefly revert to the Launching State Resolution in that limited context.

2.2 The Outer Space Treaty

As indicated before, the 1967 Outer Space Treaty is not only the most widely ratified of the space treaties, and most widely recognized as throughout representing customary international law, but also contains the structural principles regarding any activities in outer space. This applies especially in terms of Articles I and II as essentially determining the legal status of outer space as a global commons and the

---

[51] Declaration on International Cooperation in the Exploration and Use of Outer Space for the Benefit and in the Interest of all States, Taking into Particular Account the Needs of Developing Countries (hereafter Benefits Declaration), UNGA Res. 51/122, of 13 December 1996; UN Doc. A/RES/51/122. See further S. Hobe *et al.*, The 1996 Declaration on International Cooperation in the Exploration and Use of Outer Space for the Benefit and in the Interest of all States, Taking into Particular Account the Needs of Developing Countries, in *Cologne Commentary on Space Law* (Eds. S. Hobe, B. Schmidt-Tedd & K.U. Schrogl) *Vol. III* (2015), 299–362.

[52] Application of the concept of the 'launching State' (hereafter Launching State Resolution), UNGA Res. 59/115, of 10 December 2004; UN Doc. A/RES/59/115. See further M. Sánchez Aranzamendi, F. Riemann & K.U. Schrogl, The 2004 Resolution on the Application of the Concept of the 'Launching State', in *Cologne Commentary on Space Law* (Eds. S. Hobe, B. Schmidt-Tedd & K.U. Schrogl) *Vol. III* (2015), 363–400.

[53] Recommendations on enhancing the practice of States and international intergovernmental organizations in registering space objects (hereafter Registration Practice Resolution), UNGA Res. 62/101, of 17 December 2007; UN Doc. A/RES/62/101. See further B. Schmidt-Tedd, N. Hedman & A.M. Hurtz, The 2007 Resolution on Recommendations on Enhancing the Practice of States and International Intergovernmental Organizations in Registering Space Objects, in *Cologne Commentary on Space Law* (Eds. S. Hobe, B. Schmidt-Tedd & K.U. Schrogl) *Vol. III* (2015), 401–81.

[54] Recommendations on national legislation relevant to the peaceful exploration and use of outer space (hereafter National Space Legislation Resolution), UNGA Res. 68/74, of 16 December 2013; UN Doc. A/RES/68/74. See further *infra*, § 6.3.

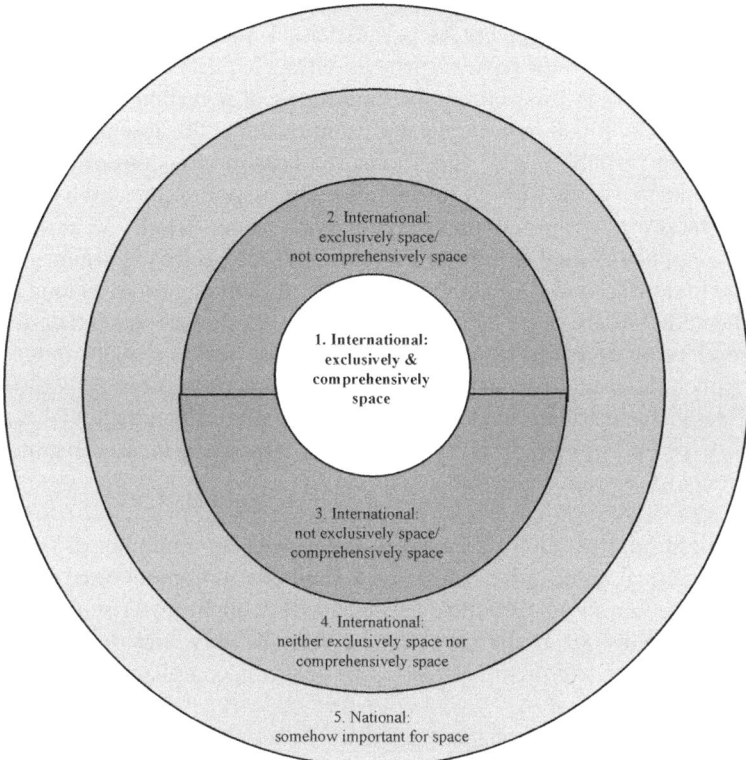

Figure 2.1 The inner core: space law *stricto sensu*

resulting baseline freedom of activity there,[55] Article III as determining that, while outer space is a special realm, general 'terrestrial' international law still (at least in principle) applies,[56] and Articles VI–VIII as spelling out the mirror side of State responsibility and liability and the need to exercise jurisdiction and control.[57]

In particular these structural principles would determine the applicability of any other regime of international space law *largo sensu*.

---

[55] See further F.G. von der Dunk, International Space Law, in *Handbook of Space Law* (Eds. F.G. von der Dunk & F. Tronchetti) (2015), 55–60; Hobe, *supra* n. 8, 25–43; Freeland & Jakhu, *supra* n. 7, 44–63.

[56] See further O. Ribbelink, Article III, in *Cologne Commentary on Space Law* (Eds. S. Hobe, B. Schmidt-Tedd & K.U. Schrogl) *Vol. I* (2009), 64–9.

[57] See further Von der Dunk, *supra* n. 55, 45–9; 51–5; Gerhard, *supra* n. 10, 103–25; Kerrest de Rozavel & Smith, *supra* n. 14, 126–45; Schmidt-Tedd & Mick, *supra* n. 16, 146–68.

The global commons character of outer space and the basic freedom of its exploration and use as per Articles I and III means that any other regime would have to provide either explicit or implicit-but-incontrovertible prohibitions or limitations of a certain kind before these can be found to be applicable as intended: in the absence of such clear-cut prohibitions or conditions, the baseline freedom of activity continues to apply without further ado. The responsibility and liability of States for private activities in outer space as per Articles VI and VII also applies if such activities are (partially) also ruled by regimes in the first or second rings, at least as a default (and of course, as long as the activities are really activities *in outer space*; downstream trade-in-services or access-to-remote-sensing-database regimes might indeed apply a different approach to private involvement in those activities). Finally, the jurisdictional tool of registration offered by Article VIII can be used for applying all sorts of originally non-space-focused regimes on board relevant spacecraft.

In addition, the Outer Space Treaty also spells out a number of broad and general substantive rules which limit the aforementioned baseline freedom in a substantive sense and thus might give rise to State responsibility, or as the case may be State liability, and the need to exercise State jurisdictional powers for ensuring compliance.

Following the nature of space activities as, certainly at the time, being highly technical, highly expensive and highly risky, the Treaty essentially focused on three main rationales for undertaking them, all typically applicable to States exclusively (and then for the first part of the space era, actually feasible for the richest and most powerful ones only): (1) military/security, as it was clear space could enhance one's military strength and thereby might be crucial to national security; (2) national prestige and the resulting international political influence (engaged in a Cold War, space was used by both superpowers to try and convince the rest of the world that their political and economic system was superior to that of the other); and (3) scientific. The substantive regime of the Outer Space Treaty, as it then largely evolved from the desire to address those three rationales and the resulting types of space activities (expected to be) undertaken, can be summarized along the following eight lines.

First, Article III, as already touched upon, provides that 'States Parties to the Treaty shall carry on activities in the exploration and use of outer space (. . .) in accordance with international law, including the

Charter of the United Nations, in the interest of maintaining international peace and security and promoting international cooperation and understanding'. This also meant that any substantive regimes, rules, principles, rights and obligations part of general international law would in principle be applicable to outer space as well, not just those pertaining to the military/security, prestige and scientific issues which were already addressed in some more detail by the Outer Space Treaty itself.

The clause is generally interpreted as a fall-back clause: wherever the specifics of space law do not provide for a clear answer to legal questions and problems, following the maxim *lex specialis derogat lege generalis*, general principles and rules of international law may sensibly be imported into the space context for determining appropriate rights and obligations.[58] Otherwise, in contrast, the *lex specialis* of the Treaty would rule: for instance, the principle of territorial sovereignty and all that it entailed, crucial to general international law, did *not* apply to outer space as a geographical area, as this was ruled out by Articles I and II of the Outer Space Treaty.

Second, at the same time of course the specific references of Article III of the Outer Space Treaty to the UN Charter and international peace and security point to the major driving factor at the time giving rise to agreement on the former: the desire to minimize the chance that the Cold War and the arms race going on would come to include outer space as another battleground. This is further corroborated by the general obligation of Article I of the Outer Space Treaty to carry out space activities 'for the benefit and in the interests of all countries', which would basically exclude all activities substantially endangering international peace and security as well.[59]

At the same time, the reference to the UN Charter clearly indicated that such principles as the prohibition on the use of force except if in self-defence or as part of UN Security Council-ordered or -mandated military operations, would at least in principle also apply to outer space.[60]

---

58 See *e.g.* Ribbelink, *supra* n. 56, 67–9.
59 As indicated, the true meaning and scope of this clause was specified and clarified by the 1996 Benefits Declaration (*supra* n. 51).
60 See Arts. 2(4), 51 & 42, UN Charter (*supra* n. 37); further on the military uses of outer space *infra*, § 4.3.

Further to that general approach, Articles IV, X and XI deal in somewhat more detail with the military aspects of the potential uses of outer space. The first Article, the most important one, notably separates the addressable realm for that purpose into outer space as a whole, respectively the Moon and other celestial bodies.

As to the first, States were committed by Article IV 'not to place in orbit around the Earth any objects carrying nuclear weapons or any other kinds of weapons of mass destruction, install such weapons on celestial bodies, or station such weapons in outer space in any other manner'. Following the general international law approach, the concept of 'weapons of mass destruction' was usually considered to refer to nuclear, biological and chemical weapons,[61] of which only the first category however seemed to be really relevant in the context of outer space. When the US government in the 1980s considered the use of laser-beam weapons as part of its Strategic Defense Initiative, a discussion raged on whether such weapons would qualify as weapons of mass destruction and hence would be prohibited or not, but as the Strategic Defense Initiative did not get beyond the drawing board, no final conclusion was (or indeed needed to be) drawn on this issue. This provision, it should be added, did *not* prohibit the placing in outer space of any weapons that were *not* weapons of mass destruction, nor did it prohibit the use of outer space as a *trajectory* for weapons of mass destruction.[62]

As to the second, States committed themselves pursuant to Article IV to use the Moon and other celestial bodies 'exclusively for peaceful purposes'. This meant in particular that

> [t]he establishment of military bases, installations and fortifications, the testing of any type of weapons and the conduct of military manoeuvres on celestial bodies shall be forbidden. The use of military personnel for scientific research or for any other peaceful purposes shall not be prohibited. The

---

61 See K.U. Schrogl & J. Neumann, Article IV, in *Cologne Commentary on Space Law* (Eds. S. Hobe, B. Schmidt-Tedd & K.U. Schrogl) *Vol. I* (2009), 75–8; also H.A. Strydom, Weapons of Mass Destruction, in *The Max Planck Encyclopedia of Public International Law* (Ed. R. Wolfrum) *Vol. X* (2012), 821–9.

62 Clearly, neither the United States nor the Soviet Union would have underwritten any treaty leading to a different result, given the importance both Cold War superpowers attached to deterrence by way of the ultimate threat to deploy their intercontinental ballistic missiles. See further F. Tronchetti, Legal Aspects of the Military Uses of Outer Space, in *Handbook of Space Law* (Eds. F.G. von der Dunk & F. Tronchetti) (2015), 335–8; Schrogl & Neumann, *supra* n. 61, esp. 75–81.

use of any equipment or facility necessary for peaceful exploration of the Moon and other celestial bodies shall also not be prohibited.[63]

It should be noted that almost all of the Soviet cosmonauts and US astronauts, certainly in the first decade of the Space Age, were indeed military personnel, notably air force, navy or marine pilots. Any provision going further than the above in terms of prohibiting all things military would thus never have carried the approval of the two major space powers.

While originally there was major disagreement on exactly how to interpret 'exclusively for peaceful purposes' (the United States reading this clause as allowing military activities as long as defensive in nature, the Soviet Union more strictly claiming this excluded all military activities except for those specifically allowed), over time the generally acknowledged proper interpretation focused on the prohibition of the threat or use of armed force in line with the UN Charter, only allowing for exceptions by way of self-defence or collective action pursuant to the UN Charter itself.[64]

The other two Articles provide for a kind of transparency- and confidence-building measures *avant la lettre*, in that reciprocal observation of space launches is urged in order to reassure that none of the above would be violated by such a launch,[65] respectively that open access to other States' stations, installations and equipment on celestial bodies was the default rule for similar purposes.[66]

Third, the value and importance of international cooperation (as a means to develop political prestige as well as reflecting the need to enhance international peace and security) has been underscored, beyond the general reference of Article III, by the provisions of Article IX addressing harmful interference with other States' legitimate activities, by far the longest substantive Article of the Treaty.[67] As to its essentials, Article IX provides:

---

63 Art. IV, Outer Space Treaty (*supra* n. 4.). See further Tronchetti, *supra* n. 62, 338–41; Schrogl & Neumann, *supra* n. 61, esp. 81–5.
64 See Arts. 51 resp. 42, UN Charter (*supra* n. 37); further *e.g.* Tronchetti, *supra* n. 62, 350–6.
65 See further A. Kapustin, Article X, in *Cologne Commentary on Space Law* (Eds. S. Hobe, B. Schmidt-Tedd & K.U. Schrogl) *Vol. I* (2009), 183–8.
66 See further J.F. Mayence & T. Reuter, Article XI, in *Cologne Commentary on Space Law* (Eds. S. Hobe, B. Schmidt-Tedd & K.U. Schrogl) *Vol. I* (2009), 189–206.
67 See further L. Viikari, Environmental Aspects of Space Activities, in *Handbook of Space Law*

In the exploration and use of outer space (...) States (...) shall be guided by the principle of cooperation and mutual assistance and shall conduct all their activities in outer space (...) with due regard to the corresponding interests of all other States (...). States (...) shall pursue studies of outer space (...) and conduct exploration of [celestial bodies] so as to avoid their harmful contamination and also adverse changes in the environment of the Earth resulting from the introduction of extraterrestrial matter and, where necessary, shall adopt appropriate measures for this purpose. If a State (...) has reason to believe that an activity or experiment planned by it or its nationals in outer space (...) would cause potentially harmful interference with activities of other States (...) in the peaceful exploration and use of outer space (...) it shall undertake appropriate international consultations before proceeding with any such activity or experiment. A State (...) which has reason to believe that an activity or experiment planned by another State (...) in outer space (...) would cause potentially harmful interference with activities in the peaceful exploration and use of outer space (...) may request consultation concerning the activity or experiment.

An even more focused requirement in this context is for States to 'agree to inform the Secretary-General of the United Nations as well as the public (...), to the greatest extent feasible and practicable, of the nature, conduct, locations and results of' activities conducted in outer space.[68]

Fourth, the scientific aspects of space activities have, beyond general references to (the importance of) exploration and use in the Preamble, Articles I and III, been given specific elaboration by way of the inclusion of 'the international scientific community' in the provision quoted above requiring States to provide relevant information, which community should by that token also be kept updated on 'the nature, conduct, locations and results of' any activities conducted in outer space by (other) States.[69]

In addition to such rationale-driven clauses, the Outer Space Treaty handles the general aims of 'exploration and use of outer space (...) for

---

(Eds. F.G. von der Dunk & F. Tronchetti) (2015), 729–31; S. Marchisio, Article IX, in *Cologne Commentary on Space Law* (Eds. S. Hobe, B. Schmidt-Tedd & K.U. Schrogl) *Vol. I* (2009), 169–82.
68 Art. XI, Outer Space Treaty (*supra* n. 4); see further Mayence & Reuter, *supra* n. 66, 195–200.
69 Art. XI, Outer Space Treaty (*supra* n. 4).

the benefit and in the interests of all countries'[70] by way of a number of cross-cutting substantive clauses.

Thus, *fifth*, the specific presence of humans in outer space (depending on the language defined as 'astronauts', 'cosmonauts' respectively whatever the appropriate legal terminology would be in Chinese, French and Spanish[71]) has been summarily addressed, as Article V requires 'States (to) regard astronauts as envoys of mankind in outer space and shall render to them all possible assistance in the event of accident, distress, or emergency landing on the territory of another State Party or on the high seas', then adding some elaborations of that generic obligation, including the requirement to 'safely and promptly' return them to the 'State of registry of their space vehicle'.[72]

As a corollary, as indicated before Article VIII subjugates those astronauts[73] to the jurisdiction of the State of registration of the space object on which they are flying, which thus can be held squarely responsible further to Article VI for activities they conduct while in outer space. Such jurisdiction extends also to astronauts while physically outside of the space objects concerned, such as when undertaking Moon walks or other extra-vehicular activities, certainly as long as such activities are of a relatively short duration only.

Sixth, as it were complementary to these clauses, a few provisions specifically deal with the inanimate 'objects' that are launched into outer space, either with or without humans on board. The aforementioned Article VIII not only offers the possibility for a State of registration of the object to extend its jurisdiction and control over that object, but also determines that the ownership thereof 'is not affected by their presence in outer space or on a celestial body or by their return

---

70 Art. I, Outer Space Treaty (*supra* n. 4); see further Hobe, *supra* n. 8, 36–8.
71 Note that as per Art. XVII, Outer Space Treaty (*supra* n. 4), the texts in those languages are equally authentic to the English and Russian versions thereof. See G.M. Goh, Articles XIV–XVII, in *Cologne Commentary on Space Law* (Eds. S. Hobe, B. Schmidt-Tedd & K.U. Schrogl) *Vol. I* (2009), 227–9.
72 See further Von der Dunk, *supra* n. 55, 79–80; F.G. von der Dunk & G.M. Goh, Article V, in *Cologne Commentary on Space Law* (Eds. S. Hobe, B. Schmidt-Tedd & K.U. Schrogl) *Vol. I* (2009), 94–102.
73 Strictly speaking, Art. VIII refers to 'personnel (...) of' 'an object launched into outer space', but this is generally interpreted as an equivalent to 'astronaut'; see further F.G. von der Dunk, Legal Aspects of Private Manned Spaceflight, in *Handbook of Space Law* (Eds. F.G. von der Dunk & F. Tronchetti) (2015), 709.

to Earth'.[74] In other words: terrestrially acquired ownership rights over such objects or their parts continue to apply also after launch. Furthermore, pursuant to Article VIII States other than the State of registry undertake to return any such object found within their grasp to the latter.

Seventh, most importantly – and somewhat uniquely – the concept of 'an object launched into outer space'[75] also triggers the substantive aspects of the international space law liability regime. While further elaborated by the Liability Convention, Article VII already provides for the fundamental requirement to somehow and at least to some extent compensate for damage caused by such objects by positing international liability for such damage.[76]

As a corollary, Article VI of the Treaty, providing for international responsibility, includes a more specific substantive obligation to assure 'that national activities are carried out in conformity with the provisions set forth in the present Treaty', which moreover in as far as such activities are conducted by 'non-governmental entities' 'shall require authorization and continuing supervision by the appropriate State Party to the Treaty', giving rise to a host of national space law regimes.[77]

Eighth, it should be noted that the Outer Space Treaty accords a particular place and role to intergovernmental organizations undertaking space activities, realizing the impossibility for most States (certainly at the time) to conduct space activities autonomously. Nevertheless, the ultimate responsibility for activities of such organizations 'shall be borne (. . .) [not only] by the international organization (. . .) [but also] by the States Parties to the Treaty participating in such organization',[78] and '[a]ny practical questions arising in connection with activities carried on by international intergovernmental organizations in the explo-

---

74 See further Von der Dunk, *supra* n. 55, 94; Schmidt-Tedd & Mick, *supra* n. 16, 163–4; and *infra*, § 2.5.
75 Art. VII, Outer Space Treaty (*supra* n. 4). *Cf.* also Von der Dunk, *supra* n. 55, 81, 86–7; Kerrest de Rozavel & Smith, *supra* n. 14, 139–40.
76 See further Von der Dunk, *supra* n. 55, 82; Kerrest de Rozavel & Smith, *supra* n. 14, 135–9; and *infra*, § 2.4.
77 See further in some detail *infra*, Chapter 6; also further Von der Dunk, *supra* n. 55, 50–5; I. Marboe, National Space Law, in *Handbook of Space Law* (Eds. F.G. von der Dunk & F. Tronchetti) (2015), 130–5; Gerhard, *supra* n. 10, 120–2.
78 Art. VI, Outer Space Treaty (*supra* n. 4); see further Gerhard, *supra* n. 10, 122–3.

ration and use of outer space (. . .) shall be resolved by the States (. . .) either with the appropriate international organization or with one or more States members of that international organization (. . .)'.[79]

In sum: the Outer Space Treaty indeed provides for a profound and all-encompassing legal framework for all humankind's endeavours in or with respect to outer space, noting at the same time that most rules are effectively rather broad and imprecise (another nickname of the Treaty is the 'Principles Treaty', shortening its actual full title which also references 'principles'). This gave rise in particular to (largely successful) efforts to elaborate and clarify especially Articles V–VIII by way of subsequent space treaties, to be addressed in the following sections.

Furthermore, in a number of instances post-1967 developments had not been foreseen at all by the Treaty's drafters, hence giving rise to major discussions on the appropriate interpretation and application of the few clauses in the Treaty that might be considered (potentially) relevant and/or applicable to them. Major examples concern the issues of space debris,[80] space mining[81] and settlements on celestial bodies.

It is important to realize, however, that none of the problems arising in this context of potential shortfalls in the Treaty's regime has led to substantial and sustained efforts to amend, let alone withdraw from, the Treaty;[82] this is a strong signal that all concerned believe they would have much more to lose by opening up the Treaty to possible amendment or even withdrawal than they might gain.[83]

2.3 The Rescue Agreement

The 1968 Rescue Agreement elaborated in particular Articles V and VIII of the Outer Space Treaty, with regard to both astronauts/personnel of a spacecraft and any space object, whether carry-

---

79 Art. XIII, Outer Space Treaty (*supra* n. 4); see further U.M. Bohlmann & G. Suess, Article XIII, in *Cologne Commentary on Space Law* (Eds. S. Hobe, B. Schmidt-Tedd & K.U. Schrogl) *Vol. I* (2009), 215–22.
80 See further *infra*, § 2.6.
81 See further *infra*, § 3.5.
82 Both of which would be permissible as per Arts. XV resp. XVI, Outer Space Treaty (*supra* n. 4); see further Goh, *supra* n. 71, 226–7.
83 See further on this issue P. Jankowitsch, The Background and History of Space Law, in *Handbook of Space Law* (Eds. F.G. von der Dunk & F. Tronchetti) (2015), 26–8.

ing astronauts or not.[84] Its substantive regime can therefore be best summarized along two lines.

First, as for astronauts the Agreement by way of Articles 1–4 outlines such general duties for States parties as to '[n]otify' both the 'launching authority' and the UN Secretary General of any accident involving 'personnel of a spacecraft',[85] to engage in reasonable 'steps to rescue them and render them all necessary assistance',[86] and to return them 'safely and promptly (. . .) to representatives of the launching authority'.[87]

With the advent of space tourism in the early 2000s, the question arose as to whether space tourists would qualify as astronauts, so as to be entitled to the same treatment under the Rescue Agreement, for instance with regard to the extent of the obligations of States to come to their rescue without regard to the costs, or to safely and promptly return them to the launching authority.[88]

Increasingly, however, such a seemingly straightforward conclusion should be questioned. While no specific legal dispute has forced the issue one way or another, in two important contexts differentiations between categories of humans in outer space have actually now been made.

The one major current international project very much focused on manned spaceflight, the International Space Station (ISS),[89] has ever since 2001 (following the visit of the first orbital space tourist Dennis Tito) created a distinction between 'astronauts' and 'spaceflight participants', the latter being defined as 'individuals (e.g. commercial, scientific and other programs; crewmembers of non-partner space agencies,

---

84 See further on the Rescue Agreement Von der Dunk, *supra* n. 55, 78–81.
85 Art. 1, Rescue Agreement (*supra* n. 30); see further Marboe, Neumann & Schrogl, *supra* n. 45, 38–47.
86 Art. 2, Rescue Agreement (*supra* n. 30), *cf.* also Art. 3; see further Marboe, Neumann & Schrogl, *supra* n. 45, 48–54.
87 Art. 4, Rescue Agreement (*supra* n. 30); see further Marboe, Neumann & Schrogl, *supra* n. 45, 59–62.
88 See for arguments for providing all humans in outer space with the status of astronauts, M.J. Sundahl, The Duty to Rescue Space Tourists and Return Private Spacecraft, 35 *Journal of Space Law* (2009), 163–200; M. Chatzipanagiotis, *The Legal Status of Space Tourists in the Framework of Commercial Suborbital Flights* (2011), esp. 5–38; essentially *contra*, however, C. Sharpe & F. Tronchetti, Legal Aspects of Public Manned Spaceflight, in *Handbook of Space Law* (Eds. F.G. von der Dunk) (2015), 647–50.
89 See further on the ISS *infra*, § 3.2.

engineers, scientists, teachers, journalists, filmmakers or tourists) sponsored by one or more partner(s). Normally, this is a temporary assignment that is covered under a short-term contract'.[90] Obviously, these distinctions would somehow also give rise to *legal* distinctions, as *inter alia* substantiated by such contracts.

Likewise, the United States, the one country that has in any detail legislated on the issue of private spaceflight including space tourism, made a similar distinction between 'crew' and 'spaceflight participant', the former being defined as 'any employee (...) who performs activities in the course of that employment directly relating to the launch, reentry, or other operation of or in a launch vehicle or reentry vehicle that carries human beings', the latter as 'an individual, who is not crew, carried within a launch vehicle or reentry vehicle', and indeed attaching some different legal consequences as between these two statuses.[91] In this case, US law has actually addressed the two categories fundamentally differently in legal terms.[92]

Second, Article 5 provides for complementary obligations of States to share information on accidents with space objects that have come to their attention and to return, as possible and relevant, any space objects or parts thereof found within their grasp, to the launching authority. The most noticeable difference is that in this case any '[e]xpenses incurred in fulfilling obligations to recover and return a space object or its component parts (...) shall be borne by the launching authority',[93] a clause entirely missing in the clauses addressing the rescue and return of astronauts.

Contrary to the clauses of the Rescue Agreement regarding astronauts, which have never been invoked (partly because the few catastrophes and near-catastrophes that have occurred in manned spaceflight

---

90 Principles Regarding Processes and Criteria for Selection, Assignment, Training and Certification of ISS (Expedition and Visiting) Crewmembers, Section III – Definitions, November 2001.
91 Sec. 50902(2) resp. (17), 51 U.S.C. See further F.G. von der Dunk, Federal *versus* State: Private Commercial Spaceflight Operator Immunity Regulation in the United States, in *Proceedings of the International Institute of Space Law 2013* (IISL) (2014), 519–20.
92 *Cf.* Sec. 50905(b)(4) resp. 505905(b)(5), 51 U.S.C., on crew resp. spaceflight participants, providing *e.g.* as for the latter a requirement of 'informed consent' before a spaceflight could be licensed. Note that more recently moreover a third category, of 'government astronaut', has been created as per Sec. 50901(15), without however as of yet giving rise to further legal specifics.
93 Art. 5(5), Rescue Agreement (*supra* n. 30); see further Marboe, Neumann & Schrogl, *supra* n. 45, esp. 70.

happened so quickly and far away that any effort at rescue or assistance would have come far too late), Article 5 on the recovery and return of space objects has regularly been invoked and applied.[94]

It is finally noteworthy that the 'launching authority', as the entity to which rescued astronauts or found space objects should be returned, also refers to an intergovernmental organization in cases where such an organization is responsible for the launching if it has complied with three further, formal preconditions, including most prominently a declaration of 'its acceptance of the rights and obligations provided for in this Agreement'.[95] In other words, by issuing such a declaration, further to the initial reference in Articles VI and XIII of the Outer Space Treaty to international organizations active in outer space, the organization in question becomes a *de facto* party to the Agreement, almost on a par with sovereign States parties.[96]

2.4 The Liability Convention

The 1972 Liability Convention elaborated Article VII of the Outer Space Treaty, as already positing the principle of international third-party liability for damage caused by objects launched into outer space. The overarching issue of whether the Liability Convention presents the sole remedy for international liability claims in the context of space activities, or whether Article VI of the Outer Space Treaty could also be invoked to claim compensation as a form of 'reparation',[97] is not addressed by either treaty, but will not be addressed here any further.[98]

---

94 See for some interesting cases K. Hodgkins, Procedures for Return of Space Objects under the Agreement on the Rescue of Astronauts, the Return of Astronauts and the Return of Objects Launched into Outer Space, in *Proceedings United Nations/International Institute of Air and Space Law Workshop on Capacity Building in Space Law* (2003), 61–6; also Lyall & Larsen, *supra* n. 11, 100–2, esp. fn. references.
95 Art. 6, Rescue Agreement (*supra* n. 30); see further Marboe, Neumann & Schrogl, *supra* n. 45, 71–4.
96 See further on this issue F.G. von der Dunk, Crossing a Rubycon? The International Legal Framework for ISOs – Before and After Privatisation, in *The Transformation of Intergovernmental Satellite Organisations* (Eds. P.K. McCormick & M.J. Mechanick) (2013), 223–9, 242–4, 247–51, 263–5; also Soucek, *supra* n. 21, 295–6.
97 *Cf.* Chorzów Factory Case; Case concerning the factory at Chorzów (Merits) (Germany v. Poland), Permanent Court of International Justice, 13 September 1928, P.C.I.J., Ser. A, No. 17, esp. 29; also Arts. 1, 2, 4–6, 8, 11, 12, 31, ILC Draft Articles on Responsibility of States for Internationally Wrongful Acts, Part 1; UN Doc. A/56/10(2001).
98 See for this issue in detail *e.g.* F.G. von der Dunk, Liability versus Responsibility in Space Law:

While the Liability Convention itself does not refer to third-party or tort liability and therefore does not fully exclude being invoked in an inter-party liability context, from its context and structure it is clear that it was meant to deal with liability towards third parties. For instance, damage on the Earth or to aircraft in flight is covered by the Convention to the extent a space object of another State is the cause thereof,[99] and similarly as to damage occurring in space itself, only damage of one space object caused by another falls within the scope of the Convention.[100]

Given the above, the regime for international third-party liability resulting from space activities as implemented by the Liability Convention consists of six main aspects to be summarized as follows.

First, a baseline liability regime is established that is almost unique in the international community. It is triggered not so much by damage caused by (space) activities as such, but by damage caused *by a space object*, which is summarily stated to 'include (. . .) component parts of a space object as well as its launch vehicle and parts thereof'.[101] While that term was not as such to be found in the Outer Space Treaty (or the Rescue Agreement for that matter), it is commonly accepted that 'space object' equates with the term 'object launched into outer space' as found in, for instance, Article VII of the Outer Space Treaty, and is ultimately to be interpreted as referring to 'any man-made object which is at least attempted to be physically brought into outer space'.[102]

This linkage of liability to damage caused by a space object in practice has been considered further limited as applying only to damage caused by kinetic interaction of that object, where damage is defined as 'loss of life, personal injury or other impairment of health; or loss of or damage to property of States or of persons, natural or juridical, or property of

---

Misconception or Misconstruction?, in *Proceedings of the Thirty-Fourth Colloquium on the Law of Outer Space* (1992), 363–71.

99 See Arts. II & VII, Liability Convention (*supra* n. 15).
100 See Art. III, Liability Convention (*supra* n. 15). Arts. IV and V provide for similar arrangements in cases where more than one launching State is involved with the space object causing the damage.
101 Art. I(d), Liability Convention (*supra* n. 15); see further Von der Dunk, *supra* n. 55, 86–7; Smith, Kerrest de Rozavel & Tronchetti, *supra* n. 45, esp. 109–10, 114–15.
102 Von der Dunk, *supra* n. 55, 87; *cf.* also Art. I(b), Liability Convention (*supra* n. 15).

international intergovernmental organizations',[103] notably excluding for instance indirect damage such as loss of revenues.[104]

Furthermore, at least as far as the Convention is concerned, liability is by definition attributed to States, to wit 'launching State[s]'; a State can qualify as such if it is either '(i) A State which launches or procures the launching of a space object; [or] (ii) A State from whose territory or facility a space object is launched'.[105] In other words, regardless of any involvement of private entities as owners, operators or service providers in any space object or the launch thereof, it is one or more States that will carry the international liability for damage caused by the space object under consideration.[106] In case indeed more than one State qualifies as a 'launching State', joint and several liability applies.[107]

As to the nature of the resulting baseline liability regime, finally a fundamental distinction is made between liability of a launching State for 'damage caused by its space object on the surface of the Earth or to aircraft in flight' which is absolute, and 'damage being caused elsewhere than on the surface of the Earth to a space object of one launching State or to persons or property on board such a space object by a space object of another launching State', where fault liability applies.[108]

Second, the Convention itself provides for a few exceptions to the applicability of its regime. Article VI allows for exoneration from absolute liability 'to the extent that a launching State establishes that the damage has resulted either wholly or partially from gross negligence

---

103 Art. I(a), Liability Convention (*supra* n. 15); see further Von der Dunk, *supra* n. 55, 84–6; Smith, Kerrest de Rozavel & Tronchetti, *supra* n. 45, esp. 105–6, 111–13.
104 Following the reference of Art. XII, Liability Convention (*supra* n. 15), to the need to 'restore the person, natural or juridical, State or international organization on whose behalf the claim is presented to the condition which would have existed if the damage had not occurred', some authors contend that actually such indirect damage *should* be included; see discussion in Smith, Kerrest de Rozavel & Tronchetti, *supra* n. 45, 111, 114–15, 126–9, 174–5; also *e.g.* B.D.K. Henaku, *The Law on Global Air Navigation by Satellite: An Analysis of Legal Aspects of the ICAO CNS/ATM System* (1998), 221.
105 Art. I(c), Liability Convention (*supra* n. 15); see further Smith, Kerrest de Rozavel & Tronchetti, *supra* n. 45, esp. 107–9, 114. See further *infra*, § 6.3 on some problems of interpretation of these definitions.
106 See further on this Von der Dunk, *supra* n. 55, 82–4.
107 See also Art. V, Liability Convention (*supra* n. 15); further Smith, Kerrest de Rozavel & Tronchetti, *supra* n. 45, 137–47.
108 Arts. II, resp. III, Liability Convention (*supra* n. 15); see further Von der Dunk, *supra* n. 55, 87–9; Smith, Kerrest de Rozavel & Tronchetti, *supra* n. 45, 116–36.

or from an act or omission done with intent to cause damage on the part of a claimant State or of natural or juridical persons it represents', whereas Article VII excludes nationals of a launching State as well as foreigners invited to be involved in a launch from the scope of the Convention as well.[109]

Third, the issue of the right to claim is addressed by the Convention itself in some detail. Article VIII provides for the baseline regime here: in order of priority, the State 'which suffers damage, or whose natural or juridical persons suffer damage', the State in whose territory the damage was sustained, and the State whose permanent residents suffered the damage have the right to assert claims under the Liability Convention.[110]

In addition, the Convention explicitly declares itself not to be an exclusive remedy in that victims of damage caused by space objects may also choose to pursue private claims 'in the courts or administrative tribunals or agencies of a launching State', which would actually suspend any claim a State is asserting or might wish to assert under the Convention itself.[111]

Fourth, the Convention provides for its own dispute settlement system. In case a claim cannot be solved through diplomatic channels and negotiations within a year,[112] either State involved may trigger the establishment of a Claims Commission as per Articles XIV–XX. These provisions on the status, role and *modus operandi* of a Claims Commission guarantee a final decision; however, such decision only 'shall be final and binding if the parties have so agreed; otherwise the Commission shall render a final and recommendatory award, which the parties shall consider in good faith'.[113] The closest these clauses came to being invoked was in the famous Cosmos-954 case, in which a Soviet nuclear-powered satellite fragmented during re-entry over

---

109 See further Smith, Kerrest de Rozavel & Tronchetti, *supra* n. 45, 148–53. The second clause also confirms that the Convention essentially addresses third-party liability.
110 Art. VIII, Liability Convention (*supra* n. 15), resp. *sub* (1), (2) and (3); further Von der Dunk, *supra* n. 55, 90–1; Smith, Kerrest de Rozavel & Tronchetti, *supra* n. 45, 154–8.
111 Art. XI(2), Liability Convention (*supra* n. 15); further Smith, Kerrest de Rozavel & Tronchetti, *supra* n. 45, esp. 167–8.
112 See Arts. XIV, IX, Liability Convention (*supra* n. 15); further Von der Dunk, *supra* n. 55, 91–2; Smith, Kerrest de Rozavel & Tronchetti, *supra* n. 45, 178–80, 159–61.
113 Art. XIX(2), Liability Convention (*supra* n. 15); further Smith, Kerrest de Rozavel & Tronchetti, *supra* n. 45, 194–7.

Canadian territory in 1978; following diplomatic negotiations the Soviet Union ultimately paid over C$3 million *ex gratia* for the damage claimed to be caused to Canada, thereby obviating the need for Canada to initiate the Claims Commission procedure.[114]

Fifth, as for the compensation, the result of Article XII is that effectively such compensation is without *a priori* limit, as it is to 'restore the person, natural or juridical, State or international organization on whose behalf the claim is presented to the condition which would have existed if the damage had not occurred'.[115] In the aforementioned Cosmos-954 case, part of the discussion regarded the question whether the compensation should also include the costs of investigation and clean-up costs; noting that the original Canadian claim amounted to over C$9 million, it may be concluded that at that point it was not agreed such costs would be included. Interestingly, 14 years later the Principles on Nuclear Power Sources, though not binding, did suggest that such costs henceforth were to be included, at least where nuclear materials would be involved: 'compensation shall include reimbursement of the duly substantiated expenses for search, recovery and clean-up operations, including expenses for assistance received from third parties'.[116]

Sixth, in terms of substantive provisions of the Convention, it bears noting that intergovernmental organizations can, as with the Rescue Agreement, effectively become parties to the Convention's rights and obligations upon compliance with three formal requirements, the most important one again being a formal declaration to that effect.[117] However, ultimately the member States of such organizations are still crucially involved directly in any dispute on liability. In case the damage is caused by a space object of an intergovernmental organiza-

---

114 *Cf.* Protocol Between the Government of Canada and the Government of the Union of Soviet Socialist Republics, done 2 April 1981, entered into force 2 April 1981; 20 ILM 689 (1981); *Space Law – Basic Legal Documents*, A.IX.2.2.2. See in more detail B.A. Hurwitz, *State Liability for Outer Space Activities in Accordance with the 1972 Convention on International Liability for Damage caused by Space Objects* (1992), 113–40; also B.A. Hurwitz, Reflections on the Cosmos 954 Incident, *Proceedings of the Thirty-Second Colloquium on the Law of Outer Space* (1990), 350–3.
115 Art. XII, Liability Convention (*supra* n. 15); further Von der Dunk, *supra* n. 55, 84–6; Smith, Kerrest de Rozavel & Tronchetti, *supra* n. 45, 172–5.
116 Princ. 9(3), Principles on Nuclear Power Sources (*supra* n. 49).
117 See Art. XXII(1), Liability Convention (*supra* n. 15); further Smith, Kerrest de Rozavel & Tronchetti, *supra* n. 45, esp. 202–5.

tion, the member States would be forced to pay the compensation due if the organization has been unable to do so within six months, whereas *vice versa* claims for compensation of damage caused to such an organization can be presented only by a member State thereof.[118]

By having thus elaborated Article VII of the Outer Space Treaty in many relevant respects, the major question arises what the legal value would be of the Liability Convention's regime for States that are party to the former but not to the latter. Given that the overwhelming majority of parties to the Outer Space Treaty have also ratified the Liability Convention and that this includes all the first-rank space powers, it would seem that the truly substantive elements of the regime (such as the definitions applied, respective applicability of absolute *versus* fault liability, joint and several liability, and the lack of a principled limit on compensation) should be deemed to also apply to those States that are party to the Outer Space Treaty but not to the Liability Convention, unless overriding arguments to the contrary can be put forward.[119] Conversely, the procedural aspects of the latter (notably the invocation of a Claims Commission) would seem to fall outside of what can be considered a mere elaboration of Article VII of the former, and hence cannot be automatically inserted by the latter into the former.[120]

2.5 The Registration Convention

The 1975 Registration Convention elaborated in particular Article VIII of the Outer Space Treaty, which had already fundamentally linked the possibility to exercise jurisdiction on a quasi-territorial basis to space objects registered by that State, by detailing the key elements of such registration. The Convention, in this respect, essentially follows a two-pronged approach.

---

118 See Art. XXII(3) resp. (4), Liability Convention (*supra* n. 15); further Smith, Kerrest de Rozavel & Tronchetti, *supra* n. 45, esp. 205–6.
119 *Cf.* also Art. 31(3), Vienna Convention on the Law of Treaties (*supra* n. 19), confirming that the interpretation of this Article in the Outer Space Treaty should take into account '(a) any subsequent agreement between the parties regarding the interpretation of the treaty or the application of its provisions; [and] (b) any subsequent practice in the application of the treaty which establishes the agreement of the parties regarding its interpretation'.
120 Contrary to the substantive provisions of the Liability Convention (*supra* n. 15), which may be seen as legal interpretation, implementation and elaboration of Art. VII, Outer Space Treaty (*supra* n. 4), these procedural clauses of the Liability Convention should therefore not be deemed to be binding customary international law; *cf.* further *supra*, n. 45.

First, it requires the 'launching State' of the space object at issue to register it in an appropriate national registry, to be established if it does not already exist, and to inform the UN Secretary-General of any establishment of such a registry.[121] The details of registration are entirely left to the State concerned.[122]

Since the launching State is defined in precisely the same manner as it has been defined in the Liability Convention,[123] sometimes more than one State would qualify as such, in which case they should among themselves agree which State would actually take the registration duties upon itself.[124] While there can be more than one launching State for any given space object, there can thus be only one State of registration. This is similar to the registration of ships or aircraft, which, resulting in the formal attribution of 'nationality' of the 'flag State' registering the vehicle, excludes the possibility of having two or more States exercise quasi-territorial jurisdiction over the vehicle concerned at the same time.[125] More problematic is that the Registration Convention does not allow for re-registration, which in view of more recent practices such as sales-in-orbit creates complicated jurisdictional situations.[126]

Second, the State of registration determined as per the above shall then provide relevant details of the space object to the UN Secretary-General for inclusion in an international register actually maintained by the UN's Office of Outer Space Affairs (UNOOSA).[127] This information, by contrast, is specifically required to at least provide, 'as soon as practicable': '(a) Name of launching State or States; (b) An appropriate designator of the space object or its registration number; (c) Date and

---

[121] See Art. II(1), Registration Convention (*supra* n. 17); further Von der Dunk, *supra* n. 55, 95–7; Schmidt-Tedd *et al.*, *supra* n. 45, esp. 251–4.
[122] See Art. II(3), Registration Convention (*supra* n. 17); further Schmidt-Tedd *et al.*, *supra* n. 45, esp. 259–61.
[123] That is, as '(i) A State which launches or procures the launching of a space object; [or] (ii) A State from whose territory or facility a space object is launched'; Art. I(a), Registration Convention (*supra* n. 17); further Schmidt-Tedd *et al.*, *supra* n. 45, esp. 244–7.
[124] *Cf.* Art. II(2), Registration Convention (*supra* n. 17); further Schmidt-Tedd *et al.*, *supra* n. 45, esp. 255–9.
[125] See for ships Arts. 91 & 92, United Nations Convention on the Law of the Sea (*supra* n. 9), for aircraft Arts. 17 & 18, Convention on International Civil Aviation (hereafter Chicago Convention), Chicago, done 7 December 1944, entered into force 4 April 1947; 15 UNTS 295; TIAS 1591; 61 Stat. 1180; Cmd. 6614; UKTS 1953 No. 8; ATS 1957 No. 5; ICAO Doc. 7300.
[126] See on this in more detail *Ownership of Satellites* (Eds. M. Hofmann & A. Loukakis) (2017), 29–162.
[127] See http://www.unoosa.org/oosa/en/spaceobjectregister/index.html (last accessed 16 June 2020).

territory or location of launch; (d) Basic orbital parameters, including: (i) Nodal period; (ii) Inclination; (iii) Apogee; (iv) Perigee; [and] (e) General function of the space object'.[128]

In addition, it may be noted that, along similar lines as with the Rescue Agreement and the Liability Convention, the Registration Convention allows intergovernmental organizations to *de facto* act as 'States' of registry, registering their space objects both internally and on the international register maintained by UNOOSA.[129]

In view of a considerable measure of lack of compliance with the Registration Convention,[130] as also demonstrated by the Registration Practice Resolution,[131] the question arises to what extent the Convention, being an elaboration in particular of Article VIII of the Outer Space Treaty, could still be argued to represent a customary international law-interpretation of that latter Article,[132] and hence apply also to States not party to the Registration Convention whilst being a party to the Outer Space Treaty.

On the one hand, the number of adherents to the Registration Convention has been steadily rising over recent years whereas no cases are known of withdrawal or even expressed intentions to withdraw, suggesting a continuing and indeed growing relevance of and adherence to the legal regime established by it. Also, the States parties include most nations with a substantial amount of space activity in outer space, potentially giving rise to registration requirements, constituting the main subject matter of the Convention's legal regime – and those *do* include all of the major spacefaring powers.

---

128 Art. IV(1), Registration Convention (*supra* n. 17); see further Von der Dunk, *supra* n. 55, 97–8; Schmidt-Tedd *et al.*, *supra* n. 45, esp. 301. Note furthermore that as per Art. IV(2) additional information *may* be added, whereas Art. IV(3) *requires*, at least 'to the greatest extent feasible and as soon as practicable', information on space objects which one way or another have deorbited.
129 *Cf.* Art. VII, Registration Convention (*supra* n. 17); further Von der Dunk, *supra* n. 55, 99; Schmidt-Tedd *et al.*, *supra* n. 45, 310–14.
130 So *e.g.* already Y. Lee, Registration of Space Objects: ESA Member States' Practice, 22 *Space Policy* (2006), 42–51.
131 *Supra* n. 53.
132 *Cf.* Art. 31(3), Vienna Convention on the Law of Treaties (*supra* n. 19): interpretation of Article VIII of the Outer Space Treaty should take into account '(a) any subsequent agreement between the parties regarding the interpretation of the treaty or the application of its provisions; [and] (b) any subsequent practice in the application of the treaty which establishes the agreement of the parties regarding its interpretation'.

Furthermore, it is recognized that '[t]he general obligation to register space objects is one of those universally accepted principles' following from the Outer Space Treaty representing customary international law, 'is in line with similar obligations for aircrafts and ships and is not a concept which is specific to this [i.e., the Registration] convention', while it should also be noted that UN Resolution 1721(B) XVI has already offered a 'soft-law' set of principles concerning registration of space objects.[133]

On the other hand, this number comprises (only) about one-third of the States in the world: while this is at least partly due to the relatively limited number of States that have launch capabilities and/or their own satellites and would therefore rather easily qualify as 'launching States' which would trigger relevant obligations under the Convention, noting that a main reason for establishment of the Convention was to help identify potentially liable States for the purposes of the Liability Convention,[134] it is still notable that a considerable majority of States of the world have *not* signed up to the Convention.[135]

Also, the many escape clauses in the Convention as to its core obligations should warn against any quick conclusion that the Convention reflects clear-cut rules of customary international law lending themselves to uniform application. Article II, dealing with national registration obligations, speaks about 'an appropriate registry', the contents of which 'shall be determined by the State of registry'.[136] Article IV, addressing States' obligations with respect to the international register, speaks about information to be provided 'as soon as practicable', optionally 'from time to time' respectively 'to the greatest extent feasible and as soon as practicable'.[137]

---

133 Schmidt-Tedd *et al.*, *supra* n. 45, 239.
134 See Schmidt-Tedd *et al.*, *supra* n. 45, 234–7.
135 It has been suggested that this might be the result of an unfortunate lack of understanding of non-launching States on the benefits of becoming a State party to the Convention (which would allow those States directly to address violations of launching States of registration-related obligations); see on this F.G. von der Dunk, The Registration Convention: Background and Historical Context, in *Proceedings of the Forty-Sixth Colloquium on the Law of Outer Space* (2003), 451–2.
136 Art. II(1), resp. (3), Registration Convention (*supra* n. 17).
137 Art. IV(1), (2) & (3) resp., Registration Convention (*supra* n. 17). Note also that the data required pursuant to Art. IV(1) are fairly limited, including merely a bland reference to the 'General function of the space object' *sub* (e).

In sum, it would seem too early to conclude that the details of the Registration Convention, even as for the substantive parts only,[138] would comprehensively constitute an interpretation of Article VIII of the Outer Space Treaty qualifying as customary international law binding also upon States not parties to the Registration Convention, certainly if not at least parties to the Outer Space Treaty. Only the general principle of registration, with a generic obligation to seriously consider both to somehow register domestically and to inform the UN Secretary-General in very general terms, might rise to that level, of being reflective of customary international law.

2.6 Space customary international law: the case of 'space debris'

While there are a number of areas in space law that are in principle relevant for all space activities where customary international law may have developed or may be developing, the one most substantial and most crucial to the development of human space endeavours, and thus meriting a brief survey here, concerns the increasing risk posed to both space operations and to Earth by way of 'space debris', that is, man-made hardware floating around in outer space without any value or function, and usually uncontrolled at that.

As space debris was not really on the political agenda in the late 1960s and early 1970s when the above four treaties were drafted, these treaties hardly provide appropriate legal tools for addressing the issue now. The Outer Space Treaty does not provide for a substantial specific obligation to avoid the creation of, or otherwise directly address, space debris,[139] the Rescue Agreement only addresses recovery duties for space objects and their fragments once found within a State's jurisdiction or control,[140] the Liability Convention only comes into play once

---

138 As before, of course, the formal clauses of Arts. VII–XII, Registration Convention (*supra* n. 17), dealing with such issues as the possibility of IGOs becoming *de facto* parties to the Convention, signature, ratification, accession, amendment and withdrawal, would not be included in the parts of the Convention reflecting customary international law in any event.
139 Art. IX, Outer Space Treaty (*supra* n. 4), only provides for an obligation to conduct exploration and use of outer space 'so as to avoid their harmful contamination', without a meaningful definition of 'harmful' as specifically including the creation of space debris, and certainly does not amount to an obligation to clear out existing space debris.
140 *Cf.* Art. 5(2) & (3), Rescue Agreement (*supra* n. 30).

space debris would cause damage as defined under the Convention[141] – presuming that the launching State(s) could be identified in the first place! – and the Registration Convention, by extending quasi-territorial jurisdiction over the space object more or less in perpetuity, even poses a substantive hurdle for States interested in clearing up other States' space debris.[142]

Over time, however, this absence of any clear-cut obligations related to the prevention of generation of new space debris and the clean-up of existing space debris became increasingly unacceptable in view of the concurrent growth of both space activities and space debris itself. While it has not been possible (yet) to draft a treaty likely to achieve widespread acceptance (or to amend an existing treaty to the same effect), developments can be discerned making it likely, or at least possible, that not too far into the future relevant customary international legal obligations would arise.

These developments really started on the international level in 2002, with the adoption by a number of major space agencies, working together in the Inter-Agency Space Debris Consultation Committee (IADC), of the first version of their Space Debris Mitigation Guidelines.[143] Constituting, indeed, guidelines for the public space agencies willing to commit themselves at an operational level, legally speaking their value was rather limited, although already based on some (albeit somewhat scattered) practice of some of those same agencies in the preceding decade. At the same time, this joint assertion by most of the world's leading space agencies of the proper approach to space debris mitigation set a clear mark on the horizon.

Once the UN's COPUOS, comprised not of space agencies but of the spacefaring States themselves, was spurred to announce a similarly oriented set of guidelines, the Space Debris Mitigation Guidelines of

---

141 Further to the commonly accepted interpretation of 'space debris' being included in the concept of 'space object', *cf.* Arts. I(a) & (d), II–V, Liability Convention (*supra* n. 15). See on this further Smith, Kerrest de Rozavel & Tronchetti, *supra* n. 45, 115; Viikari, *supra* n. 67, 736.
142 *Cf.* the combined effects of Art. VIII, Outer Space Treaty (*supra* n. 4) and Arts. I(a) & (c), IV, Registration Convention (*supra* n. 17).
143 In 2007 these guidelines were updated; see IADC Space Debris Mitigation Guidelines; A/AC.105/C.1/L.260. See further Viikari, *supra* n. 67, 749–52; P. Stubbe et al., The 2007 Space Debris Mitigation Guidelines of the Committee on the Peaceful Uses of Outer Space, in *Cologne Commentary on Space Law* (Eds. S. Hobe, B. Schmidt-Tedd & K.U. Schrogl) *Vol. III* (2015), 614–15, 624–5.

the Committee on the Peaceful Uses of Outer Space, in its first iteration in 2007,[144] the value of such voluntary guidelines as a standard-setting agreement to combat space debris was elevated to a political and proto-legal level. It was not yet binding, but possibly – hopefully – preparing the ground and leading the way towards the actual creation of customary international law.

Despite occasional drawbacks, such as most recently the Indian ASAT-test,[145] the effect has already been that a number of individual major spacefaring States now use these guidelines in their domestic processes for licensing private space operators – as obligations binding upon them.[146] If this process is going to continue, and to include even more major spacefaring nations, soon indeed a uniform State practice-*cum-opinio iuris* might come to be discerned effectively reflecting the essence of the IADC and COPUOS guidelines, giving rise to norms of customary international law.

Unfortunately, these developments only address the mitigation of generation of new space debris, by including obligations for instance to minimize on-orbit break-ups and desist from intentional break-ups such as ASAT tests. They are so far not addressing (nor were they, politically and legally speaking, able to address) the other generic aspect of space debris mitigation: clearing out existing debris, hopefully before it starts creating (yet more) damage.[147] In the latter area in particular, therefore, a lot still remains to be achieved.

2.7 Concluding remarks

While the four UN treaties discussed above are the only treaties unequivocally falling within the inner core of the *corpus iuris spatialis internationalis* as defined, with customary international law such a

---

144 See A/AC.105/890, Annex IV, A/62/20; also UN OOSA (2010), ST/SPACE/49. See further Viikari, *supra* n. 67, 741–6; Stubbe *et al., supra* n. 143, 605–52.
145 See https://en.wikipedia.org/wiki/2019_Indian_anti-satellite_missile_test (last accessed 16 June 2020).
146 This concerns *e.g.* the United States, Japan, France, Italy and the United Kingdom; see L. Viikari, *The Environmental Element in Space Law* (2008), 96.
147 On this, see further Viikari, *supra* n. 67, 757–9, ff.; also *e.g.* M.P. Schaefer, Analogues Between Space Law and Law of the Sea/International Maritime Law: Can Space Law Usefully Borrow or Adapt Rules from These Other Areas of Public International Law?, in *2012 Proceedings of the International Institute of Space Law* (2013), 316–30.

determination is less clear-cut. The issue of space debris clearly stands out as the most important one not dealt with by the space treaties as well as currently developing in the hoped-for direction of becoming customary international law, but almost by definition customary international law is very difficult to delineate in terms of substantive matter.

This is partly the consequence of the all-encompassing nature of the Outer Space Treaty coupled with the very general and broad character of its clauses and principles. Even in the case of space debris, which presents a substantive topic of its own yet relevant to all space activities *and* not addressed in any helpful measure by the text of the Outer Space Treaty itself, the customary legal developments discussed above can ultimately be related to the general principles of the Treaty on the use and exploration of outer space for all humankind, on international cooperation and on efforts to avoid harmful interference.

It is thus testimony to the farsightedness of the Treaty's drafters that there is hardly any subject matter of importance for today's space endeavours which cannot be traced back, one way or another, to clauses to be found within the Treaty. At the same time, of course, most clauses and principles contained in the Treaty are, indeed, very broad and general, so much so as to often provide little specific answer as to how major issues arising later would have to be legally addressed at the international level.

While in a first phase of space law's development some of those could be addressed by three further treaties, as discussed above, once the fourth, the Moon Agreement, failed to attract much ratification (certainly of major space powers), it was largely left to customary international law, whether or not supported by authoritative UN Resolutions, to try and develop helpful rules, rights and obligations in furtherance of the broad and general aims of the Outer Space Treaty.[148]

Beyond the issue of space debris, perhaps the most vexing fundamental legal questions not addressed by the Outer Space Treaty in sufficient detail relate to the on-going privatization of space activities (which,

---

148 See on this *e.g.* S. Hobe, The Relevance of Current International Space Treaties in the 21st Century, 27 *Annals of Air and Space Law* (2002), 335–46; S. Hobe, Space Law – An Analysis of its Development and its Future, in *Outer Space in Society, Politics and Law* (Eds. C. Brünner & A. Soucek) (2011), 476–89; P. Jankowitsch, The Role of the United Nations in Outer Space Law Development: Past Achievements and New Challenges, 26 *Journal of Space Law* (1998), 101–10.

nevertheless, have to ultimately look for answers further to relevant clauses of the Treaty such as Articles VI and VII), to the issue of military usage of outer space (where, in contrast, non-space law such as the UN Charter and the law of armed conflict are drawn into the discussion) and to the possible exploitation of valuable resources (whether radio spectrum and orbits where the ITU regime has traditionally taken the lead role, or mineral resources where most stakeholders are still groping for appropriate legal regimes to apply by analogy).

What *is* certain, however, is that even such paradigm-changing developments will and indeed will have to take place within the parameters of the inner core of space law as discussed in this chapter – the alternative would be far more worrying. Fortunately, up till now, at least all key stakeholders agree to that evaluation. While this does not present a guarantee that outer space will remain free from major conflicts or major mishaps, legally speaking it clarifies that, indeed, this core body of the *corpus iuris spatialis internationalis* represents a *lex specialis*, requiring in principle all other relevant legal regimes, from the rings around the core, to fit within its main parameters.

3 The 'Northern' part of the first ring of space law

3.1 Introduction

Contrary to the inner core of international space law which essentially comprises four treaties and some customary international law largely interwoven with at least the Outer Space Treaty, a large number of treaties would belong in the Northern part of the first ring of Figure 3.1 as containing all international law very much focused on outer space and space activities yet not addressing all of them even in principle, as well as a much broader range of areas subject to customary international law.

For instance, many bilateral and multilateral treaties deal with specific, almost *ad hoc* instances of international cooperation on space activities. Bilateral agreements can deal with a wide range of subjects, from the provision of launch services by one country to another country[149] or to an intergovernmental organization,[150] to broader cooperation agreements on launches,[151] space sciences[152] or astronaut training.[153]

---

149 *E.g.*, Agreement between the Government of Australia and the Government of the United States of America concerning the furnishing of Launch and Associated Services for Australia's National Satellite System, Washington, done 7 March 1985, entered into force 7 March 1985; ATS 1985 No. 7.

150 *E.g.*, Agreement between the Government of the Commonwealth of Australia and the European Space Research Organisation for the Provision and Operation of Trials Facilities at Woomera for Launching of a SKYLARK Rocket in January/February 1970, Paris, done 10 January 1970, entered into force 10 January 1970; ATS 1970 No. 1.

151 *E.g.*, Treaty between the Government of the Russian Federation and the Government of the Republic of Kazakhstan on the Leasing of the Baikonur-Complex, done 10 December 1994; *Biulleten mezhdunarodnych dogovorov 1998 No. 10*, 9–16.

152 *E.g.*, Framework Agreement between the Government of the People's Republic of China and the Government of the Federative Republic of Brazil on Cooperation in the Peaceful Applications of Outer Space Science and Technology, Beijing, done 8 November 1994, entered into force 29 June 1998; 2036 UNTS 335.

153 *E.g.*, Agreement concerning the Training of Mission Specialists for Space Shuttle Flights, with implementing agreement [Canada & United States], Ottawa, done 31 August 1995 & 17 May 1996; entered into force 17 May 1996; 2028 UNTS 133.

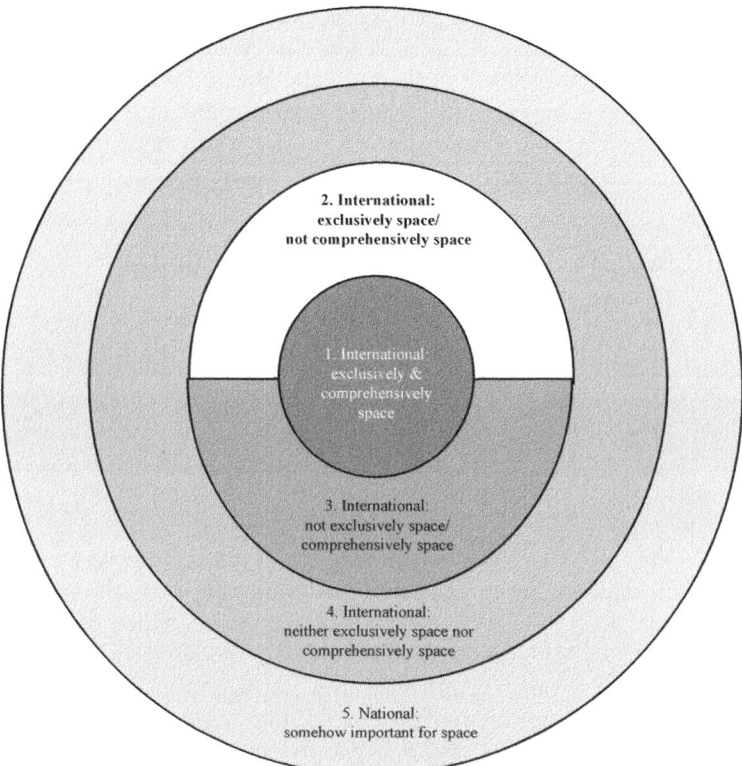

Figure 3.1 The 'Northern' part of the first ring of space law

Multilateral treaties may address specific elements of the space environment, such as the potentially unauthorized onward transmission of satellite signals[154] or even the establishment of full-fledged intergovernmental organizations active in outer space.[155]

At this point, however, analysis will focus first on the few major multilateral treaties with several major spacefaring countries on board as well as addressing major space projects, namely the Intergovernmental

---

154 E.g., Convention relating to the Distribution of Programme-carrying Signals Transmitted by Satellite, Brussels, done 21 May 1974, entered into force 25 August 1979; 1144 UNTS 3; TIAS 11078; ATS 1990 No. 30; 13 ILM 1444 (1974).
155 E.g., Agreement for Cooperation in the Exploration and Use of Outer Space for Peaceful Purposes (INTERCOSMOS), Moscow, done 13 July 1976, entered into force 25 March 1977; 16 ILM 1 (1977).

Agreement on the ISS, the ITSO Agreement, the IMSO Convention and the ESA Convention. In addition, the Moon Agreement will be addressed in view of its special role as the last of the UN-originating space treaties being currently debated in the context of space mining, as well as, finally, the area of remote sensing where some important norms of customary international law have arisen.

3.2 The Intergovernmental Agreement on the International Space Station

There is little question that the step-by-step construction, launch, maintenance and operation of an international space station in Low-Earth Orbit was the single most challenging space enterprise since the Moon landings – and legally speaking the most challenging full stop.[156]

Currently 15 States have ratified the 1998 Intergovernmental Agreement providing the fundamental legal regime for all activities concerning the ISS,[157] including the two initial space superpowers and erstwhile Cold War enemies the United States and Russia (as successor to the Soviet Union). The other Partner States are Canada and Japan, longstanding political allies of the United States, as well as 11 European States working together also for this project through the European Space Agency (ESA) of which they are members.[158]

The whole enterprise of constructing and launching the ISS step by step, and then maintaining and operating it, was explicitly confirmed to comply with the core space law regime offered by the Outer Space Treaty, the Rescue Agreement, the Liability Convention and the Registration Convention, as well as more generally with international

---

156 See further S. Rosmalen, The International Space Station Past, Present and Future – An Overview, in *The International Space Station* (Eds. F.G. von der Dunk & M.M.T.A. Brus) (2006), 9–32; M. Berlingheri, A Policy and Legal Framework for Commercial Utilisation, in *The International Space Station* (Eds. F.G. von der Dunk & M.M.T.A. Brus) (2006), 33–46; W. Ley & W. Stoffel, Report of the 'Project 2001' Working Group on Space Stations, in *'Project 2001' – Legal Framework for the Commercial Use of Outer Space* (Ed. K.H. Böckstiegel) (2002), 330–49.
157 Many of the details were worked out in Memoranda of Understanding between the space agencies involved and further implementing arrangements; see Art. 4, Intergovernmental Agreement on the ISS (*supra* n. 32).
158 This concerned Belgium, Denmark, France, Germany, Italy, the Netherlands, Norway, Spain, Sweden, Switzerland and the United Kingdom.

law.[159] In other words, wherever the States parties in the Agreement deviated from that regime, that was only as between themselves; yet even so they took that regime generally to provide the baseline for the specific regime on the ISS as between the parties.

Further to the provisions of Article VIII of the Outer Space Treaty and the Registration Convention (notably Article II(2)), the individual modules comprising the space station (and, as for Canada, the Mobile Servicing System, essentially a giant and very sophisticated robotic arm) were agreed to be registered by the relevant States that had built and owned and operated them, with the further understanding that ESA, acting as the space agency of the 11 participating European States and having complied with the conditions of Article VII of the Registration Convention,[160] acts as the 'State' of registry of the European module.[161]

This means further that in line with the same provisions of the space law treaties each State of registry 'shall retain jurisdiction and control over the elements it registers', but then the Intergovernmental Agreement on the ISS deviates from those provisions by allocating potential exercise of jurisdiction and control 'over personnel in or on the Space Station *who are its nationals*', as opposed to those who are 'of' the particular module concerned.[162]

Then, recognizing also that ESA, not being a sovereign State, could not exercise and therefore 'retain jurisdiction' in the legal sense of the word in any event,[163] the rules on jurisdiction were elaborated beyond this general allocation in two areas considered of major importance for the proper development and operation of the ISS.

---

159 See Art. 2(1), Intergovernmental Agreement on the ISS (*supra* n. 32).
160 Art. VII, Registration Convention (*supra* n. 17), provides that 'references to States shall be deemed to apply to any international intergovernmental organization which conducts space activities if the organization declares its acceptance of the rights and obligations provided for in this Convention and if a majority of the States members of the organization are States Parties to this Convention and to the Treaty on Principles Governing the Activities of States in the Exploration and Use of Outer Space, including the Moon and Other Celestial Bodies'. See also *supra*, text at n. 129.
161 As per Art. 5(1), Intergovernmental Agreement on the ISS (*supra* n. 32).
162 Art. 5(2), Intergovernmental Agreement on the ISS (*supra* n. 32); emphasis added. Note that Art. VIII, Outer Space Treaty (*supra* n. 4) extends potential exercise of jurisdiction and control to the State of registry of a space object also 'over any personnel thereof'.
163 See further A. Farand, Jurisdiction and Liability Issues in Carrying out Commercial Activities in the International Space Station (ISS) Programme, in *The International Space Station* (Eds. F.G. von der Dunk & M.M.T.A. Brus) (2006), 87–95.

On the one hand, on intellectual property rights, key to the main aim of the ISS to serve as a unique laboratory for developing new products and technologies, Article 21 used the (quasi-)territorial criterion: States were entitled to apply their domestic intellectual property right laws to the respective modules they had registered. In the absence of ESA having any 'territory' in the legal sense, it was further provided that 'for ESA-registered elements any European Partner State may deem the activity to have occurred within its territory'.[164]

On the other hand, on criminal jurisdiction Article 22 by contrast applied the nationality criterion: at a first level, all participating States 'may exercise criminal jurisdiction over personnel in or on any flight element who are their respective nationals',[165] noting that European astronauts do not lose their individual nationality merely by being in the service of ESA. At a second level, also States (otherwise) affected by the alleged misconduct may become engaged in exercising criminal jurisdiction, if the State holding primary rights would allow for that.[166]

Another fundamental area where the ISS partners first apply rules of the international space law regime, but then adapt them for *inter se* purposes, concerns liability for damage. Thus, the parties officially confirm that the liability regime of Article VII of the Outer Space Treaty and the Liability Convention continues to apply, both *vis-à-vis* non-partner States to the ISS and among themselves *as long as not in the context of 'Protected Space Operations'*.[167]

However, as for those Protected Space Operations (PSOs), broadly defined as 'all launch vehicle activities, Space Station activities, and payload activities on Earth, in outer space, or in transit between Earth and outer space in implementation of this Agreement, the MOUs, and implementing arrangements',[168] instead of imposing or accepting any liabilities the Partner States agree to a very broad cross-waiver of liability, not only between themselves, but also as between 'any of the entities or persons' fundamentally involved in such PSOs and with

---

164 Art. 21(2), Intergovernmental Agreement on the ISS (*supra* n. 32). Note that so far Germany and Italy have actually done so; see A.M. Balsano & J. Wheeler, The IGA and ESA: Protecting Intellectual Property Rights in the Context of ISS Activities, in *The International Space Station* (Eds. F.G. von der Dunk & M.M.T.A. Brus) (2006), 67–9; Ley & Stoffel (*supra* n. 156), 347–8.
165 Art. 22(1), Intergovernmental Agreement on the ISS (*supra* n. 32).
166 *Cf.* Art. 22(2), Intergovernmental Agreement on the ISS (*supra* n. 32).
167 *Cf.* Art. 17, Intergovernmental Agreement on the ISS (*supra* n. 32).
168 Art. 16(2)(f), Intergovernmental Agreement on the ISS (*supra* n. 32).

only very limited exceptions, and furthermore agree to ensure that all such entities and persons indeed are formally brought to accept that cross-waiver.[169]

In conclusion, the Intergovernmental Agreement on the ISS, as supported by a range of further legal and semi-legal documents, provides for a legal structure controlling the most complex space project since the start of the Space Age by essentially taking the inner core of space law as its baseline, and then building upon it and/or only deviating from it when this was specifically called for.

3.3 The ITSO Agreement and the IMSO Convention

Following the rapid development of technologies in the 1960s allowing for the inclusion of satellites in telecommunication networks with global coverage, the enormous financial costs and risks involved in establishing the relevant satellite infrastructure gave rise to the establishment of two intergovernmental organizations pooling the technical and financial resources of the respective sets of member States for the purpose. Those organizations obviously were based on quite elaborate legal frameworks, limited both in scope *ratione personae* (namely to the respective sets of member States) and in scope *ratione materiae* (namely to the respective categories of satellite communication services).

INTELSAT was established in 1971 to create such an organization mainly for 'fixed satellite services', that is services between terrestrial transmitters fixed on the ground using satellites. Next, INMARSAT was established in 1976 to achieve the same for what at the time were maritime services, but later on more generally came to encompass all 'mobile satellite services', that is services using satellites involving terrestrial transmitters of which at least one was mobile.

Both organizations in that sense were clear examples of the provision of Article I of the Outer Space Treaty, that 'outer space should be used for the benefit and in the interests of all countries',[170] and that

---
169 See Art. 16(3), Intergovernmental Agreement on the ISS (*supra* n. 32).
170 Preamble, Agreement Relating to the International Telecommunications Satellite Organization (INTELSAT) (hereafter INTELSAT Agreement), Washington, done 20 August 1971, entered into force 12 February 1973; 1220 UNTS 21; TIAS 7532; 23 UST 3813; UKTS 1973 No. 80; Cmnd.

further to Article III of that Treaty international cooperation was to be considered a preferable, very effective and practical means to achieve such ambitions.

Both organizations, being open at least in principle to all States worldwide,[171] were established along the same lines, creating in effect hybrid public consortia.

The States parties ratified the INTELSAT Agreement,[172] respectively INMARSAT Convention,[173] the highest legal documents in each case setting out the general structure, roles and competences of the two organizations, whereas the actual telecom operators (at the time usually public entities, hence labelled 'Public Telecommunication Operators', PTOs), one per State party, became signatories to the INTELSAT Operating Agreement,[174] respectively INMARSAT Operating Agreement,[175] in each case detailing the further approach to operations and relevant rights and responsibilities pertaining to the use of the respective space segments.

The most unique feature of both these organizations (which was also copied in a more limited European context by EUTELSAT, established in 1982[176]), was the complex mechanism by which the contributions

---

4799; ATS 1973 No. 6; 10 ILM 909 (1971); as well as Preamble, Convention on the International Maritime Satellite Organization (INMARSAT) (hereafter INMARSAT Convention), London, done 3 September 1976, entered into force 16 July 1979; 1143 UNTS 105; TIAS 9605; 31 UST 1; UKTS 1979 No. 94; Cmnd. 6822; ATS 1979 No. 10; 15 ILM 1052 (1976).

171 Note that the Soviet Union, though having refused to join INTELSAT as being considered too much dominated by the United States, did join INMARSAT in view of its overarching interests in being part of a global satellite system used for search and rescue purposes; cf. F. Lyall, INMARSAT, in *The Max Planck Encyclopedia of Public International Law* (Ed. R. Wolfrum) Vol. V (2012), 205–7.

172 *Supra*, n. 170.

173 *Supra*, n. 170.

174 Operating Agreement Relating to the International Telecommunications Satellite Organization (INTELSAT) (hereafter INTELSAT Operating Agreement), Washington, done 20 August 1971, entered into force 12 February 1973; 1220 UNTS 149; TIAS 7532; 23 UST 4091; UKTS 1973 No. 80; Cmnd. 4799; ATS 1973 No. 6; 10 ILM 946 (1971).

175 Operating Agreement on the International Maritime Satellite Organization (INMARSAT) (hereafter INMARSAT Operating Agreement), London, done 3 September 1976, entered into force 16 July 1979; 1143 UNTS 213; TIAS 9605; 31 UST 1; UKTS 1979 No. 94; Cmnd. 6822; ATS 1979 No. 10; 15 ILM 233, 1075 (1976).

176 As per the Convention Establishing the European Telecommunications Satellite Organization (EUTELSAT), Paris, done 15 July 1982, entered into force 1 September 1985; UKTS 1990 No. 15; Cm. 956; Cmnd. 9069; *Space Law – Basic Legal Documents*, C.II.1; and the Operating Agreement

of the various member States through their PTOs were balanced on an annual basis with the corresponding level of usage of the satellite capacity by those PTOs.[177] This business-like approach ensured that both organizations developed into major success stories of international cooperation: in 2000, INTELSAT counted 143 member States and operated 17 satellites in geostationary orbit; for INMARSAT those numbers were 87, respectively 10.[178]

By that time, however, the world economy, satellite technology and the service markets had changed to such an extent that pressure was mounting, in particular in the United States, Europe, Japan, Canada and Australia, to commercialize and privatize the provision of satellite communication services.[179] On the other side of the fence, however, there were many countries, in particular developing ones, which were afraid that in the process of commercialization and privatization the major public services which INTELSAT and INMARSAT had offered, comprising the most prominent and visible manifestations of the ambitions to implement the lofty goals of Article I of the Outer Space Treaty, would come to be quickly neglected or even abolished.[180]

Relating to the European Telecommunications Satellite Organization (EUTELSAT), Paris, done 15 July 1982, entered into force 1 September 1985; UKTS 1990 No. 15; Cm. 956; Cmnd. 9154; *Space Law – Basic Legal Documents*, C.II.2.

177 See Art. V, INTELSAT Agreement (*supra* n. 170) and Arts. 4, 6, 7, INTELSAT Operating Agreement (*supra* n. 174); resp. Art. 5, INMARSAT Convention (*supra* n. 170), and Arts. III, V, VI, INMARSAT Operating Agreement (*supra* n. 175).

178 See F.G. von der Dunk, International Organizations in Space Law, in *Handbook of Space Law* (Eds. F.G. von der Dunk & F. Tronchetti) (2015), 283–7, 290–3.

179 Such pressures, in legal terms, were reflected by the WTO quickly after 1994 becoming engaged in satellite communication services (see further *infra*, § 5.4), the Satellite Directive (Commission Directive amending Directive 88/301/EEC and Directive 90/388/EEC in particular with regard to satellite communications, 94/46/EC, of 13 October 1994; OJ L 268/15 (1994)) initiating the privatization of satellite communications within Europe and the ORBIT Act (Open-market Reorganization for the Betterment of International Telecommunications Act, 17 March 2000, Public Law 106-80, 106th Congress) doing the same for the United States; see further P.K. McCormick, Neo-Liberalism: A Contextual Framework for Assessing the Privatisation of Intergovernmental Satellite Organisations, in *The Transformation of Intergovernmental Satellite Organisations* (Eds. P.K. McCormick & M.J. Mechanick) (2013), 1–34; also D. Sagar, Privatization of the International Satellite Organizations, in '*Project 2001*' – *Legal Framework for the Commercial Use of Outer Space* (Ed. K.H. Böckstiegel) (2002), 501–9; U.M. Bohlmann, K.U. Schrogl & I. Zilioli, Report of the 'Project 2001' Working Group on Telecommunication, in '*Project 2001*' – *Legal Framework for the Commercial Use of Outer Space* (Ed. K.H. Böckstiegel) (2002), 218–20.

180 See M.J. Mechanick, The Role and Function of Residual International Intergovernmental Satellite Organisations Following Privatisation, in *The Transformation of Intergovernmental Satellite Organisations* (Eds. P.K. McCormick & M.J. Mechanick) (2013), 176–81.

Ultimately, the forces pressing for privatization turned out to be irresistible, and in 2000 all operations of INTELSAT were handed to a newly created company Intelsat (based in Washington, where INTELSAT had its headquarters);[181] and likewise all operations of INMARSAT had been handed already in 1998 to a newly created company Inmarsat (based in London, where INMARSAT had its headquarters).[182] Both companies still count among the largest satellite service operators in the world.

However, in the process of privatization the lofty goals of Article I of the Outer Space Treaty were not entirely forgotten. While the former intergovernmental organizations (IGOs) shrunk to ITSO (the new acronym for 'International Telecommunication Satellite Organization'), respectively IMSO (the new acronym for 'International Mobile Satellite Organization'), these two IGOs were reconstituted as watchdogs to ensure that the two private operators would continue to provide the original public functions most dear to the international community, as legally entrenched in contracts between the oversight IGOs and the private operators which the latter could not unilaterally change or terminate.

Thus, under a Public Service Agreement ITSO had the oversight authority to ensure that Intelsat would continue to comply with 'Lifeline Connectivity Obligations' (referring to those States who depended upon the Intelsat system for most or all of their international communications) for at least 12 years from the date of privatization onwards, subject to the same prices and other key parameters as before, as well as to obligations to maintain global connectivity and global coverage and non-discriminatory access to the satellite system.[183] Under a similar Public Service Agreement IMSO would guarantee that Inmarsat would continue to provide the Public Service Obligations, of which the continued operation of the Global Maritime Distress and Safety System (GMDSS) was the most important one, at the same level

---

181 See further P.K. McCormick, Intelsat: Pre- and Post-Private Equity Ownership, in *The Transformation of Intergovernmental Satellite Organisations* (Eds. P.K. McCormick & M.J. Mechanick) (2013), 81–117; Von der Dunk, *supra* n. 178, 287–90.
182 See further D. Sagar & P.K. McCormick, Inmarsat: In the Forefront of Mobile Satellite Communications, in *The Transformation of Intergovernmental Satellite Organisations* (Eds. P.K. McCormick & M.J. Mechanick) (2013), 35–79; Von der Dunk, *supra* n. 178, 293–5.
183 Pursuant to Art. III, Agreement Relating to the International Telecommunications Satellite Organization (ITSO), Washington, done 20 August 1971, entered into force 12 February 1973, as amended 13 November 2000, amended version entered into force 30 November 2004; Cm. 5092; *Space Law – Basic Legal Documents*, C.V.1.

as hitherto, at least until another entity would take care thereof at the same conditions.[184]

While the application of these new structures has not been without controversies and (at least) political disputes, it is important to note that these two institutional constructs continue to play a major role in efforts to guarantee continued availability of crucial public services. ITSO as of today comprises 149 member States, many of which still benefit from the 'Lifeline Connectivity' which the system offers,[185] whereas IMSO has grown to a membership of 104 States, continuing to guarantee and enjoy access to the GMDSS.[186]

3.4 The ESA Convention

While INTELSAT and INMARSAT offered the two most important examples of a large number of spacefaring nations pooling financial and other resources for very specific and focused space-related operations in intergovernmental organizations underpinned by elaborate legal frameworks, ESA offers the premier example of a group of nations[187] pooling such resources for a wide array of space and space-related activities, as long as they fall within the remit of its constitutive document, the ESA Convention.

That remit was outlined as follows: 'The purpose of the Agency shall be to provide for and to promote, for exclusively peaceful purposes, cooperation among European States in space research and technology and their space applications, with a view to their being used for scientific purposes and for operational space applications systems'.[188] This directly echoes provisions of the Outer Space Treaty such as calling for 'activities in the exploration and use of outer space [to be] (...) in the

---

[184] See Art. 2(1), Public Service Agreement Between the International Mobile Satellite Organization and Inmarsat One Limited and Inmarsat Two Company; pursuant to Arts. 3, 4, Convention on the International Mobile Satellite Organization, London, done 3 September 1976, entered into force 16 July 1979, as amended 1998, amended version entered into force 31 July 2001; ATS 2001 No. 11.
[185] *Cf.* https://itso.int/about-us/ (last accessed 16 June 2020) and https://itso.int/about-us/mission-role/ (last accessed 16 June 2020).
[186] *Cf.* https://imso.org/imso-today/ (last accessed 16 June 2020).
[187] Currently, ESA comprises 22 member States plus a number of cooperating States in various formalized contexts; see https://en.wikipedia.org/wiki/European_Space_Agency (last accessed 16 June 2020).
[188] Art. II, ESA Convention (*supra* n. 35).

interest of maintaining international peace and security and promoting international cooperation and understanding'.[189]

The Agency's legal framework based on the Convention has provided for a flexible yet coherent institutional and operational cooperative environment, crucially by providing strong incentives for its member States to 'Europeanize' any space activities within the above remit they might consider undertaking and *vice versa* join any such space activities indeed conducted by ESA.[190]

The Convention in this respect provides for two key categories of activities. On the one hand, mandatory activities, normally concerning basic science and research and development usually in a terrestrial environment, once adopted by the ESA Council (consisting of member State representatives) by simple majority, are to be funded jointly by *all* member States (including those opposing), with individual member State contributions calculated as per an objectivized scale reflecting average national income.[191] This reflects the cooperative spirit: if States are not even willing to submit to an obligation to contribute funds to such programmes following a majority decision in the Council, the question should be asked why they would be – should be – members of an organization like ESA in the first place.

On the other hand, optional activities, often concerning launches and major satellite operations in outer space, allow for the level of *à la carte* flexibility required from an intergovernmental organization consisting of sovereign member States. Also optional activities require a simple majority of member States in the Council to be adopted, but they allow (1) for an opt-out of individual member States not interested in participating, and, for those States that do participate, (2) deviation from the standard distribution of the budget following national income otherwise applicable.[192]

---

189 Art. III, Outer Space Treaty (*supra* n. 4).
190 Note that the ESA Director General, apart from exercising functions of a more executive and representative nature, has the authority to 'submit proposals concerning activities and programmes as well as measures designed to ensure the fulfilment of the Agency's purpose' (Art. XII(1)(b), ESA Convention (*supra* n. 35)); many programmes carried out by ESA have indeed resulted from such proposals (as opposed to individual member States proposing such programmes for ESA to undertake).
191 See Arts. V(1)(a), XI(5)(a)(i), XIII(1), ESA Convention (*supra* n. 35). Mandatory activities overall average some 15% of the Agency's total programme budgets.
192 See Arts. V(1)(b), XI(5)(c)(i), XIII(1), ESA Convention (*supra* n. 35). Optional activities overall average some 85% of the Agency's total programme budgets.

A major stimulus for indeed substantially contributing to optional activities finally is provided by a main principle of the industrial policy principle underpinning ESA, 'that all Member States participate in an equitable manner, having regard to their financial contribution'.[193] This fundamental principle is further elaborated in Annex V on Industrial Policy by the so-called 'geographical distribution' or 'fair return' clause, stipulating that '[i]n the placing of all contracts, the Agency shall give preference to industry and organisations of the Member States. However, within each optional programme covered by Article V.1 (b) of the Convention, particular preference shall be given to industry and organisations in the participating States'.[194] Even more precisely, '[i]deally the distribution of contracts placed by the Agency should result in all countries having an overall return coefficient of 1',[195] meaning each country should ideally speaking see a proportion of ESA contracts revert to its national industry which matches the proportion that country contributed, as much as possible per individual programme, but certainly in an overall sense.

Along the above lines, ESA became a major contributor not only to the global efforts in space science and research and development,[196] but also to the further promotion of the regime developed by the space law treaties. Uniquely, it complied with the conditions for intergovernmental organizations to become *de facto* parties to the Rescue Agreement,[197] the Liability Convention[198] and the Registration Convention.[199]

---

193 Art. VII(1)(c), ESA Convention (*supra* n. 35).

194 Art. II(1), Annex V, ESA Convention (*supra* n. 35).

195 Art. IV(3), Annex V, ESA Convention (*supra* n. 35).

196 It should be noted that the Agency is generally restrained from providing space services on a routine, (quasi-)commercial basis; whenever its research, technology development and experimental activities resulted in a practical application, the Agency created 'daughter' entities to run those applications on a daily basis: Arianespace for launch services; EUTELSAT, later Eutelsat, for satellite communications; and EUMETSAT for satellite weather forecasting. See further F.G. von der Dunk, European Space Law, in *Handbook of Space Law* (Eds. F.G. von der Dunk & F. Tronchetti) (2015), 227–38.

197 As per Art. 6, Rescue Agreement (*supra* n. 30); for the relevant Declaration of 1975, see *International Organisations and Space Law* (Ed. R.A. Harris) (1999), 25.

198 As per Art. XXII, Liability Convention (*supra* n. 15); for the relevant Declaration of 1976, see *International Organisations and Space Law*, *supra* n. 197, 33.

199 As per Art. VII, Registration Convention (*supra* n. 17); for the relevant Declaration of 1979, see *International Organisations and Space Law*, *supra* n. 197, 27.

While – fortunately – it has not been necessary yet to invoke the Rescue Agreement and Liability Convention, as for the latter a Resolution of 1977 was nevertheless already adopted to spell out how any particular claim for liability under the Liability Convention would be effectively shared between the various member States.[200] As for the Registration Convention, the role of ESA as launching 'State' of many space objects has given rise to, at the time of writing, 90 ESA entries in the UNOOSA register.[201] In particular, of course, as discussed in greater detail above, further to the arrangements regarding the ISS as per the Intergovernmental Agreements where ESA acted as the joint space agency of the 11 European Partner States, ESA registered the European module.[202]

ESA furthermore is one of the original founding member space agencies of the Inter-Agency Space Debris Consultative Committee (IADC), thus sharing a leading role in developing guidelines, standards and norms for addressing space debris.[203] Noting that several major space powers, notably France, the United Kingdom, Germany and Italy, are member States of ESA, any standard and uniform compliance by the Agency with such guidelines, standards and norms might be viewed as a form of 'collective' State practice developing in the context of an emerging norm of customary international law on the issue.[204]

3.5 The Moon Agreement and space mining

The 1979 Moon Agreement was concocted as, following the Moon landings of 1969–1972, it was expected that soon more permanent facilities would be built there *inter alia* to start exploring for, and if successful exploiting, mineral resources found there, and it was (rightly)

---

200 See Resolution on the Agency's Legal Liability, ESA/C/XXII/Res. 3, adopted Paris, 13 December 1977; *International Organisations and Space Law, supra* n. 197, 35.
201 See https://www.unoosa.org/oosa/osoindex/search-ng.jspx (last accessed 16 June 2020).
202 See *supra* at § 3.2. More in detail on the legal aspects of ESA involvement in the ISS, *e.g.* R.P. Veldhuyzen & T.L. Masson-Zwaan, ESA Policy and Impending Legal Framework for Commercial Utilisation of the European Columbus Laboratory Module of the ISS, in *The International Space Station* (Eds. F.G. von der Dunk & M.M.T.A. Brus) (2006), 47–62; also Balsano & Wheeler, *supra* n. 164, 63–86.
203 See further *supra* at § 2.6.
204 See on this issue more in general T. Treves, Customary International Law, in *The Max Planck Encyclopedia of Public International Law* (Ed. R. Wolfrum) *Vol. II* (2012), 946–8; Von der Dunk, *supra* n. 178, 309–17.

perceived that the Outer Space Treaty would require elaboration in this respect.[205] Thus, the Agreement which ultimately resulted, apart from reiterating and to some extent reinforcing or detailing a number of general provisions of the Outer Space Treaty with regard to the Moon and other celestial bodies,[206] in a number of clauses addressed the possibilities of such future exploitation.

The umbrella provision in this regard stated that the 'Moon and its natural resources are the common heritage of mankind', as elaborated in further provisions of the Moon Agreement.[207] These included in particular the aim 'to establish an international regime, including appropriate procedures, to govern the exploitation of the natural resources of the Moon as such exploitation is about to become feasible'.[208] Such a regime in turn was supposed to guarantee

(a) The orderly and safe development of the natural resources of the Moon;
(b) The rational management of those resources;
(c) The expansion of opportunities in the use of those resources; [and]
(d) An equitable sharing by all States Parties in the benefits derived from those resources, whereby the interests and needs of the developing countries, as well as the efforts of those countries which have contributed either directly or indirectly to the exploration of the Moon, shall be given special consideration.[209]

While, owing largely to the relative lack of specificity of those provisions (how strict and detailed would such an 'international regime' have to be in order to qualify?) and how the 'common heritage of mankind' principle was to play out exactly, the text was originally adopted without much controversy, this changed rapidly after final agreement on that text.[210] Most prominently, it turned out that in the concurrent drafting of the overarching 1982 United Nations Convention on

---

205 See S. Hobe *et al.*, The 1979 Agreement Governing the Activities of States on the Moon and Other Celestial Bodies, in *Cologne Commentary on Space Law* (Eds. S. Hobe, B. Schmidt-Tedd & K.U. Schrogl) *Vol. II* (2013), esp. 336–41.
206 *Cf. e.g.* Arts. 3 (on peaceful purposes), 4 (on exploration and use being the province of all mankind), 6 (on the freedom of scientific investigation), Moon Agreement (*supra* n. 31).
207 Art. 11(1), Moon Agreement (*supra* n. 31). See in general F. Tronchetti, *The Exploitation of Natural Resources of the Moon and Other Celestial Bodies* (2009), 85–130; Hobe *et al.*, *supra* n. 205, 336–7, 345–7, 388–99.
208 Art. 11(5), Moon Agreement (*supra* n. 31).
209 Art. 11(7), Moon Agreement (*supra* n. 31).
210 See in detail Tronchetti, *supra* n. 207, 99–110, also *e.g.* 225.

the Law of the Sea the 'common heritage of mankind' principle *was* elaborated in quite some detail with regard to the looming possibility to mine the deep seabed, up to obligatory transfer of technology, effective sharing of material benefits from such mining operations, and a supranational institution-*cum*-enterprise construct ensuring compliance with both.[211]

This was unacceptable to most of the developed States, which in the context of the law of the sea refused to ratify the United Nations Convention on the Law of the Sea – and then, assuming that any future international regime for the Moon would likely be developed along the same lines, also rallied against the Moon Agreement (followed in that latter context, it should be said, by the absence of ratification by most other countries as well). As a result, the Moon Agreement as of today carries only 18 ratifications, of which perhaps only Australia would qualify as a space power of some stature.[212]

For many years this remained a largely theoretical issue. However, then, fairly recently, a few US companies became engaged in serious and far-reaching preparatory plans to mine asteroids, essentially as 'celestial bodies' equated to the Moon in legal terms. This ignited a debate as regards the extent to which a single State could proceed to authorize such private commercial mining operations, or whether conversely an international regime of considerable substance would be called for prior to any such operation becoming legal, which would follow from the most common interpretation of the 'common heritage of mankind'.

In the absence of applicability of the Moon Agreement and its use of that concept of the 'common heritage of mankind' (other than for the States parties to it) however, recourse needs to be had to the Outer Space Treaty, which merely provided for a prohibition of 'national

---

211 See esp. Arts. 136–137, 150–185, United Nations Convention on the Law of the Sea (*supra* n. 9); also *e.g.* Hobe *et al.*, *supra* n. 205, 390–1.
212 While, in addition, France and India are among the signatories of the Moon Agreement (*supra* n. 31), thereby in principle subject to the obligation 'not to defeat the object and purpose' thereof pursuant to Art. 18, Vienna Convention on the Law of Treaties (*supra* n. 19), their signatures by now are decades old, and neither nation has since then shown any intention to actually become a party. Given furthermore that the Agreement does not allow for a possibility to 'un-sign', only to withdraw *after* ratification (*cf.* Art. 20), fairly little legal meaning would seem to attach to those signatures nowadays.

appropriation [of celestial bodies] by claim of sovereignty, by means of use or occupation, or by any other means'.[213]

Some States (and others) tried to argue that this basic provision included a prohibition on national appropriation of any resources in outer space, in particular mineral ones, sometimes by simply equating the 'province of all mankind' of Article I of the Outer Space Treaty to the 'common heritage of mankind' of the Moon Agreement,[214] sometimes by arguing that the absence of success of the Moon Agreement equated with the absence of *any* regime allowing mineral resource exploitation, thus effectively resulting in a prohibition thereof.[215]

In contrast, the United States, Luxembourg and the United Arab Emirates, the three countries which so far have unilaterally adopted national laws allowing private space mining activities subject to a licence and compliance with applicable international law,[216] argued that mineral resource exploitation should not be compared with resource exploitation of the deep seabed (where the strict and very detailed regime of the United Nations Convention on the Law of the Sea referenced above applied), but to resource exploitation of the high seas (where the same Convention reconfirmed the basic freedom of the high seas as including resource exploitation[217]).

To the extent an international regime might be warranted to protect certain general interests of the international community and humankind, just as with regard to commercial exploitation of radio frequencies and orbital slots, the need for such a regime would not exclude the principal sovereign right of States to license particular private companies for the purpose, as part of the broader freedom of

---

213 Art. II, Outer Space Treaty (*supra* n. 4).
214 *Cf. e.g.* Tronchetti, *supra* n. 207, 44; Hobe *et al.*, *supra* n. 205, 364–7, 394–5.
215 *Cf. e.g.* Tronchetti, *supra* n. 207, 43; Hobe *et al.*, *supra* n. 205, 396–7.
216 Title IV, U.S. Commercial Space Launch Competitiveness Act (hereafter Commercial Space Launch Competitiveness Act); Public Law 114–90, 114th Congress, 25 November 2015; 51 U.S.C. 513; Law on the exploration and utilization of space resources (*Loi du 20 juillet 2017 sur l'exploration et l'utilisation des ressources de l'espace*); of 20 July 2017, published 28 July 2017; http://legilux.public.lu/eli/etat/leg/loi/2017/07/20/a674/jo (last accessed 16 June 2020); resp. Federal Law No. 12 of 2019 on the Regulation of the Space Sector, of 19 December 2019; https://www.moj.gov.ae/assets/2020/Federal%20Law%20No%2012%20of%202019%20on%20 THE%20REGULATION%20OF%20THE%20SPACE%20SECTOR.pdf.aspx (last accessed 16 June 2020).
217 See Art. 87, United Nations Convention on the Law of the Sea (*supra* n. 9).

use of outer space pursuant to Article I of the Outer Space Treaty as mirrored by the State responsibility of Article VI for any such licensed private activities. Interestingly, even the Moon Agreement itself only prohibited national appropriation of 'natural resources *in place*',[218] at least suggesting that natural resources post-extraction *could* be appropriated.

While political resistance against unilateral licensing has not (yet) disappeared, at the time of writing it seemed that the focus was shifting to efforts to ensure that any private space mining activities to be licensed by the United States, Luxembourg, the United Arab Emirates and probably others would be subjected to more substantive rules on such issues as non-harmful interference, liability for damage to the environment and other public interests as part of the international law to which also those countries had pledged they would hold their private operators.[219]

In sum, the main legal discussion centres around the assumption that Article II of the Outer Space Treaty only disallows appropriation of 'territory' in outer space as such, not necessarily the *use* of such 'territory' even if for commercial exploitation purposes, as being a form of 'use' addressed by the freedom of exploration and use of Article I of the Treaty. Efforts to import the concept of a 'common heritage of mankind' as prominently proposed by the Moon Agreement into the Outer Space Treaty, and the suggestions that this should mean that only an international licensing regime could legitimize commercial mineral exploitation, seem to fail both for lack of adherence to the former as opposed to the latter, and for lack of compatibility of such an international regime with the freedom of use and exploration propounded by the Outer Space Treaty. Ultimately, therefore, these arguments are based more on political considerations than on proper legal analysis.

---

218 Art. 11(2), Moon Agreement (*supra* n. 31); emphasis added.
219 *Cf.* also the agreements Luxembourg has entered into not just with the United States, but also with China, Japan, the United Arab Emirates, the Czech Republic, Portugal, Poland and Belgium. See *e.g.* https://today.rtl.lu/news/science-and-environment/a/1296733.html (last accessed 16 June 2020); http://www.spacedaily.com/reports/Luxembourg_and_Belgium_join_forces_to_develop_space_resources_999.html (last accessed 16 June 2020).

3.6 The UN Principles on Remote Sensing and customary international law

A final element of the Northern part of the first ring worthy of attention here concerns the efforts to develop international law specifically on satellite remote sensing. After the failure of the Moon Agreement to attract the participation of more than a few States as discussed above, the efforts to create new law on topical issues of outer space became less ambitious, and focused on the adoption of UN General Assembly Declarations with the hope that these would sooner or later come to reflect customary international law.[220]

One of those issues concerned the increasing possibilities of using satellite remote sensing for sounding out terrestrial opportunities for mineral resource mining, which arose in the 1970s and 1980s, giving rise to worries in particular with developing States being sensed that the developed States sensing them would use the knowledge gained for their own economic purposes, in addition to worries that data which could alleviate suffering and destruction in humanitarian crises would not be made readily and/or freely available.[221]

Following a long lead time where originally the intention indeed had been to draft a proper treaty, in 1986 the UN Principles on Remote Sensing[222] were adopted, mainly with a view to addressing the above concerns. Consequently, the Principles focused very much on acknowledging the two major legal arguments put forward, both based on the Outer Space Treaty, including its Article III as referencing general public international law, and then trying to reconcile them.

On the one hand, the developing States, at the time generally not enjoying their own independent access to satellite remote sensing data, argued that the unquestioned sovereignty over national territory and the natural resources therein[223] should also include sovereignty over

---

220 See Hobe, The Relevance, *supra* n. 148, 335–46; Von der Dunk, *supra* n. 55, 39–43.
221 See F. Tronchetti, Legal Aspects of Satellite Remote Sensing, in *Handbook of Space Law* (Eds. F.G. von der Dunk & F. Tronchetti) (2015), esp. 507 ff.; J. Gabrynowicz *et al.*, The 1986 Principles Relating to Remote Sensing of the Earth from Outer Space, *Cologne Commentary on Space Law* (Eds. S. Hobe, B. Schmidt-Tedd & K.U. Schrogl) *Vol. III* (2015), 86–7, 162–9.
222 *Supra* n. 48. See further Tronchetti, *supra* n. 221, 517–25; Gabrynowicz *et al.*, *supra* n. 221, 81–188.
223 Further to Art. 2(1), UN Charter (*supra* n. 37), as recognized also in Princ. IV, Principles on Remote Sensing (*supra* n. 48); see further *e.g.* S. Marchisio, Remote Sensing for Sustainable

data concerning national territory and its natural resources. Such sovereignty should ideally require prior consent of the sensed State to any satellite operation remote sensing its territory, subsidiary an exclusive, free or at least preferential right of access to the data resulting from such an operation.

On the other hand, the sensing States, essentially comprising only developed nations, counterargued that the freedom of space activity as expressed by Article I of the Outer Space Treaty, further underpinned by the baseline freedom of generation of information which was part of general international law,[224] precluded any such right of 'prior consent', or even exclusive, free and/or preferential right of access.

The Principles reflected an elaborate effort to reconcile both positions. For instance, Principle IV prominently asserts both, without addressing cases where the two cannot apply at the same time and one of the two has to be accorded priority over the other:

> Remote sensing activities shall be conducted in accordance with the principles contained in *article I* of the Treaty on Principles Governing the Activities of States in the Exploration and Use of Outer Space, including the Moon and Other Celestial Bodies, which, in particular, provides that the exploration and use of outer space shall be carried out *for the benefit and in the interests of all countries*, irrespective of their degree of economic or scientific development, and stipulates the principle of *freedom of exploration and use of outer space on the basis of equality*. These activities shall be conducted on the basis of *respect for the principle of full and permanent sovereignty of all States and peoples over their own wealth and natural resources*, with due regard to the rights and interests, in accordance with international law, of other States and entities under their jurisdiction. Such activities shall not be conducted in a manner detrimental to the *legitimate rights and interests of the sensed State*.[225]

In the end, however, when access to remote sensing data had to be addressed, a choice had to be made. Following an initial definition

---

Development in International Law, in *Outlook on Space Law over the Next 30 Years* (Eds. G. Lafferranderie & D. Crowther) (1997), esp. 341–2.

224 As also recognized in Princ. IV, Principles on Remote Sensing (*supra* n. 48); see further *e.g.* M. Williams, The UN Principles on Remote Sensing Today, in *Proceedings of the Forty-Eighth Colloquium on the Law of Outer Space* (2006), 2–4; Marchisio, *supra* n. 223, 335–40.

225 Princ. IV, Principles on Remote Sensing (*supra* n. 48); emphasis added. See also Tronchetti, *supra* n. 221, 521–3; Gabrynowicz *et al.*, *supra* n. 221, 114–16.

of 'primary data',[226] 'processed data'[227] and 'analysed information',[228] the cardinal clause of the Principles states:

> As soon as the primary data and the processed data concerning the territory under its jurisdiction are produced, the sensed State shall have access to them on a non-discriminatory basis and on reasonable cost terms. The sensed State shall also have access to the available analysed information concerning the territory under its jurisdiction in the possession of any State participating in remote sensing activities on the same basis and terms, taking particularly into account the needs and interests of the developing countries.[229]

In other words, first, as for the primary and processed data neither a right of 'prior consent', nor exclusive, free and/or preferential rights to the data on a sensed State for that State were recognized, only its right of access on a 'non-discriminatory basis', and then again only 'on reasonable cost terms'. This right, however, includes both data generated by a sensing State itself (for instance by its national space agency) and data generated by private operators operating under its responsibility as per Article VI of the Outer Space Treaty.[230]

Second, as for analysed information, the right of access of a sensed State to remote sensing data concerning its own territory is limited even further, namely only to those 'in the possession of any State participating in remote sensing activities', and then (again) 'on the same basis and terms'.[231] Private operators investing in developing such analysed information as the key product or service of their business plan,

---

226 Princ. I(b), Principles on Remote Sensing (*supra* n. 48), defines 'primary data' as 'raw data that are acquired by remote sensors borne by a space object and that are transmitted or delivered to the ground from space by telemetry in the form of electromagnetic signals, by photographic film, magnetic tape or any other means'.
227 Princ. I(c), Principles on Remote Sensing (*supra* n. 48), defines 'processed data' as 'the products resulting from the processing of the primary data, needed to make such data usable'.
228 Princ. I(d), Principles on Remote Sensing (*supra* n. 48), defines 'analysed information' as 'the information resulting from the interpretation of processed data, inputs of data and knowledge from other sources'.
229 Princ. XII, Principles on Remote Sensing (*supra* n. 48). See also Tronchetti, *supra* n. 221, 523–4; Gabrynowicz *et al.*, *supra* n. 221, 162–9.
230 See also Princ. XIV, Principles on Remote Sensing (*supra* n. 48), which almost verbatim repeats the clause of Art. VI, Outer Space Treaty (*supra* n. 4), in this context.
231 Princ. XII, Principles on Remote Sensing (*supra* n. 48). See also Tronchetti, *supra* n. 221, 523–4; Gabrynowicz *et al.*, *supra* n. 221, 162–9.

therefore, are basically entitled to market and sell such information pursuant to standard commercial principles as they see fit.

The hope that the Principles on Remote Sensing would indeed provide a fruitful point of departure towards customary international law regarding satellite remote sensing (at least in the somewhat limited area dealt with by the Principles, that is 'sensing of the Earth's surface from space by making use of the properties of electromagnetic waves emitted, reflected or diffracted by the sensed objects, *for the purpose of improving natural resources management, land use and the protection of the environment*'[232]) was strengthened by the fact that, differently from the preceding major UN Resolution on space, the Principles on Direct Broadcasting by Satellite,[233] these Principles were adopted by consensus. Consensus is generally defined as 'the absence of any objection expressed by a representative and submitted by him as constituting an obstacle to the taking of the decision'.[234]

This did not necessarily mean, however, that the ambiguity still perceived with regard to some of the principles was completely solved as well. Some authors in particular interpreted the key phrase of Principle XII on 'access on a non-discriminatory basis' as providing first for a right of access which should then somehow be shaped in a non-discriminatory fashion.[235] A first problem with such an interpretation, however, is that the second part of the key phrase would effectively come to be without meaning: if it cannot qualify the right of access by allowing for denial of access as long as on a non-discriminatory basis, there is no need to add that qualification in any event. A second one would be that major spacefaring States would be very unlikely to have consented to even a non-binding UN resolution if they would have understood it as essentially requiring them to give a sensed State access to data generated by them which, even if generated 'for the purpose of improving natural resources management, and use and the protection of the environment' pursuant to Principle I(a), might also have strategic, military or other national security implications and value.

---

232 Princ. I(a), Principles on Remote Sensing (*supra* n. 48); emphasis added. See also Gabrynowicz et al., *supra* n. 221, esp. 95–7.
233 See *supra* n. 47.
234 Rule 69, Final Recommendation of the Helsinki Consultations of the Conference on Security and Co-operation, as quoted in R. Wolfrüm & J. Pichon, Consensus, in *The Max Planck Encyclopedia of Public International Law* (Ed. R. Wolfrum) Vol. II (2012), 673.
235 *Cf. e.g.* Gabrynowicz et al., *supra* n. 221, 167.

More importantly than what individual authors, experts or not, including the present author, surmise or argue, however, is of course how the States concerned, in particular leading sensing States and leading sensed States, interpret and implement this principle. From a succinct analysis of the data access legislation and policies of the major sensing States a strong argument arises that 'access on a non-discriminatory basis' could legitimately mean that (1) no access would need to be provided at all to the sensed State, as long as it was also not provided to other States (after all, in such an event there would not be 'discrimination'); or even more importantly, that (2) 'on a non-discriminatory basis' would still legitimize 'discriminating' between other States that contributed to the satellite remote sensing operation and those that did not, or that offered something in return which others did not, and even (3) would legitimize 'discriminating' more generally between political allies and others.[236]

In addition, it could now be safely stated that the erstwhile highly visible political controversy underlying the discussion has lost much of its relevance as a consequence of political, technical and commercial developments in the sector since the 1980s. Several leading developing States have now crossed the line from being only sensed States to undertaking major sensing operations themselves, such as China, India and Brazil,[237] thereby diluting to a large extent the somewhat unified interests of the developing world as they were perceived in 1986. In addition, technical developments driving down costs at the same time as improving quality have allowed for a commercial remote sensing sector to arise (although admittedly still in somewhat fledgling fashion), thereby offering many sensed States not in a position to become sensing States themselves the possibility to gain access to remote sensing data at much more reasonable prices in any event, diluting their urge for an international legal *obligation* to do so.

---

236 See *e.g.* the analysis in Tronchetti, *supra* n. 221, 525–41, discussing in particular the United States, Canada, Germany, France, China, Brazil, India and Japan; on ESA and EUMETSAT early on, F.G. von der Dunk, Non-Discriminatory Data Dissemination in Practice, in *Earth Observation Data Policy and Europe* (Ed. R. Harris) (2002), 43–6.

237 *Cf.* Tronchetti, *supra* n. 221, 508–12; A. Ito, *Legal Aspects of Satellite Remote Sensing* (2011), 10–12, 94–6; R. Harris, Science, Policy and Evidence in EO, in *Evidence from Earth Observation Satellites* (Eds. R. Purdy & D. Leung) (2013), 43; R.A. Williamson, Legal and Policy Issues in Satellite Remote Sensing, in *'Project 2001' – Legal Framework for the Commercial Use of Outer Space* (Ed. K.H. Böckstiegel) (2002), 165–77.

3.7 Concluding remarks

As indicated, this chapter has only dealt with the few most important international legal regimes belonging to the Northern part of the first ring. In each of those cases, it becomes clear that while they were, at least potentially, able to deviate from the rules of the core of the *corpus iuris spatialis internationalis*, this was applicable at best between the respective sets of parties – and even then, the four international treaties discussed in Chapter 2 were usually followed as a baseline, default regime; deviation was only considered where specific circumstances legitimized such deviations. For instance, the Intergovernmental Agreement on the ISS by changing the inter-party liability regime to one of a cross-waiver chose not to transplant the Liability Convention's fault liability regime to its specific context in order to honour the general spirit of international cooperation.

The Outer Space Treaty in particular served as, and was explicitly recognized to be, a basis for both the International Space Station and the European Space Agency as peaceful endeavours; the post-privatization international satellite organizations were specifically charged with preserving overarching interests of humankind at large in an otherwise privatized and commercialized environment; and the ongoing discussion on the legality of space mining centres around a proper interpretation of Articles I and II of the Treaty.

Furthermore, the ISS used the Registration Convention's pointers to structure the competing exercise of jurisdiction by the States parties; ESA honoured the possibilities offered by three of the four treaties to become a *de facto* party to their regimes; and even the Moon Agreement, although far from widely ratified, has played a role in shaping the discussion on space mining.

From one perspective this may seem to be a turnaround regarding the *lex specialis–lex generalis* analysis – after all, the Intergovernmental Agreement on the ISS, the ITSO Agreement, the IMSO Convention, the ESA Convention and even the Moon Agreement are all *leges speciales* compared with the *lex generalis* of in particular the Outer Space Treaty – *but only as between parties to the former*.

In addition, the fact that actually the former set of treaties (just like the multitude of treaties, multilateral as well as bilateral, falling in the Northern part of the first ring referred to above[238] but not addressed here in any further detail) all pay heed to the latter, testifies to the overarching and very fundamental character of the Outer Space Treaty and its closest offspring, the Rescue Agreement, the Liability Convention and the Registration Convention, which are presumably not to be deviated from even among limited sets of States at least unless profoundly different rationales apply.

---

238 See *supra*, § 3.1.

4 The 'Southern' part of the first ring of space law

4.1 Introduction

The Southern part of the first ring comprises a number of international regimes containing international law more or less directly relevant for all space activities, yet not very much focused on them (Figure 4.1). While Article III of the Outer Space Treaty[239] simply pronounces that in a sense *all* international law not specifically targeting outer space activities could yet be part of space law in a broader sense, the Southern part of the first ring only concerns that part thereof at least visibly and sensibly applicable to *all* space activities – not, for instance, to the satellite communications sector only, such as the international trade regime established under the WTO, or to the private commercial manned spaceflight sector only, such as international air law.

Furthermore, it should be reiterated that Article III is commonly interpreted as defining international space law as a *lex specialis* with reference to the *lex generalis* of international law at large, which means that the latter only comes into play in the context of outer space or space activities to the extent that space law itself is moot or fundamentally open to conflicting interpretations.[240] In other words, for any rule of international law that does not derive from the inner core or the Northern part of the first ring to be applicable in a space context requires it to fit within whatever that inner core, subsidiary the Northern part of the first ring to the extent applicable, provides as boundary parameters.

From this vantage point, three major regimes in the Southern part of the first ring stand out as being so important that, somehow, they even partially escape the limitations of the above, albeit for different reasons and on different legal grounds: the international regime addressing

---
239 See further *supra*, § 2.2.
240 See also *supra*, text at ns. 12, 28.

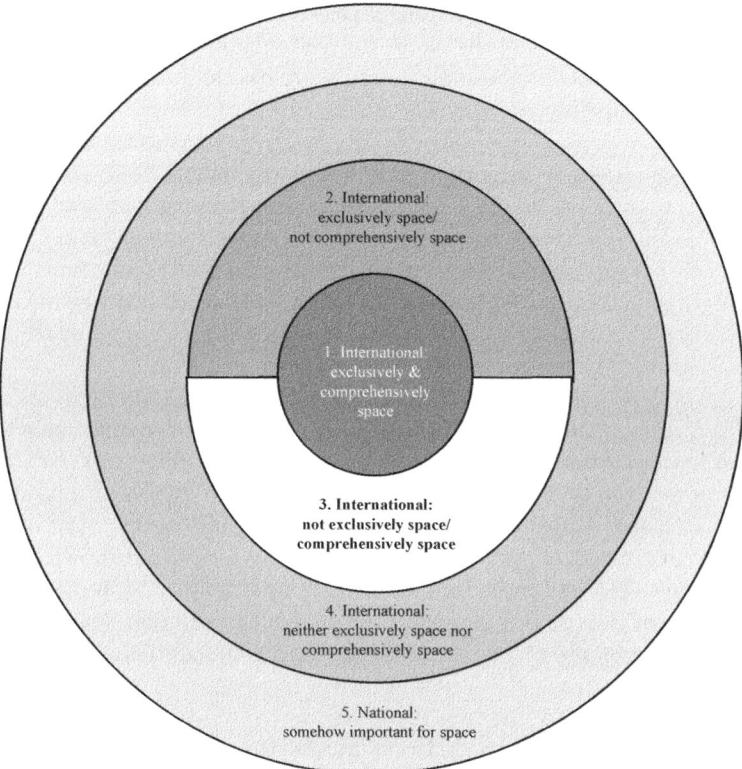

Figure 4.1 The 'Southern' part of the first ring of space law

the international use of radio frequencies as developed in the context of the ITU, the body of international law addressing the use of armed force in the international community and the international regimes addressing dual-use security-sensitive technology exports as closely related to relevant dedicated national legal regimes.

4.2 The international regime on the international use of radio frequencies in space

Almost as soon as technological developments allowed the use of more advanced means than talking and writing for intra-human communications, the potential possibilities and ramifications also for long-distance, including as relevant international, communications became visible. The International Telecommunication Union (ITU), not accidentally one of the oldest truly international intergovernmental organizations, was established in 1865 basically to address those ramifications.[241]

At first limited to telegraph technology (originally, 'ITU' stood for 'International Telegraph Union'), it soon came to encompass also wireless communication technologies using the radio frequency spectrum. In other words, in the context of ITU an international regime handling international communications had already been developed well before the possibilities became apparent of using satellites in outer space as part of the infrastructure used for such communications.[242]

It was only in 1957, following *Sputnik-1*, that the ITU system came to be confronted with the need to address the use of radio waves to communicate with extra-terrestrial objects, soon to include astronauts and cosmonauts. At the World Administrative Radio Conference (WARC) of 1959, consequently, the ITU member States formally acknowledged that the ITU was the appropriate body to handle the international aspects of the use of radio waves in the context of outer space, integrating them into the larger operational environment of long-distance communications.

The first aspect that needs to be understood is that in that context radio waves soon came to be used for two fundamentally different purposes.

One was the need to control any space object operating in outer space, that is for ground control stations to be fed with information on its 'status' and position, in order to then allow, as necessary, adjustments to its operational parameters in outer space such as a change of orbit or a change of speed. This is generally required for *all* space activities, manned or unmanned, and is commonly known as telemetry, tracking and control (TT&C) operations.

---

[241] See further https://en.wikipedia.org/wiki/International_Telecommunication_Union (last accessed 16 June 2020). Also F. Lyall, *International Communications – The International Telecommunication Union and Universal Postal Union* (2011), 17–212; D. Westphal, International Telecommunication Union (ITU), in *The Max Planck Encyclopedia of Public International Law* (Ed. R. Wolfrum) *Vol. VI* (2012), 166–76.

[242] The earliest moment that serious thought was given to the possibility of using relay satellites in space for communication purposes was the seminal 1945 paper of Arthur C. Clarke, Extra-Terrestrial Relays, *Wireless World* (Oct. 1945), 305–8.

In addition, depending upon their exact function, satellites needed further commands to do what they were sent into outer space for in the first place. Remote sensing satellites might need to be commanded to turn or focus their cameras on a particular part of the Earth's surface and then to transmit the resulting images back; navigation satellites need their emitted time signals to be regularly calibrated and updated in order to make positioning by triangulation possible; and scientific satellites need to be made to send down the results of the experiments undertaken up there. While all these functions are generally speaking not considered 'satellite communications', they all need access to frequencies without interference in order to operate as desired.[243]

The other concerns 'satellite communications' properly speaking, which requires the use of frequencies to transmit communication messages (that is, 'messages' other than images, time signals or scientific results). Here, satellites are part of an enormous infrastructure spanning the globe, also consisting of many ground stations using radio waves or wired (copper, glass fibre and other) technologies, and their use as part of a telecommunications network essentially depends on trade-offs between costs and benefits as compared with other technologies – a trade-off that constantly changes owing to the ebb and flow of relative technological changes and innovations in all domains concerned.

Consequently, the ITU had to fit the specific use of satellite frequencies within the general international regulatory regime developed for allowing the use of frequencies for telecommunications without harmful interference. The core elements of that regime were, first, a recognition 'that radio frequencies and any associated orbits, including the geostationary-satellite orbit, are limited natural resources that must be used rationally, efficiently and economically, in conformity with the provisions of the Radio Regulations',[244] and second, a complex and flexible system for coordination of the intended use of frequencies and attendant orbits avoiding interference as much as possible.

---

243 Note that in the context of the ITU some frequency bands are even reserved for radio astronomy; in order for scientists to be able to 'listen in' to the radio emissions from dying stars, black holes and supernovas, such frequencies are not to be used for other purposes if potentially interfering with such scientific activities. *Cf.* Art. 1.58, ITU Radio Regulations (2016), https://www.itu.int/en/publications/ITU-R/pages/publications.aspx?parent=R-REG-RR-2016&media=electronic (last accessed 16 June 2020).

244 Art. 44(2), ITU Constitution (*supra* n. 36).

That system in turn consisted of two, alternatively three steps.

The first step concerned 'allocation', which refers to the 'reservation' at the international level of frequency *bands* to *categories* of services using radio waves.[245] While originally, in 1959, only a 'space service' (the 'uplink' to the satellite) and an 'earth service' (the 'downlink' from the satellite) were defined as separate services, and in 1971 a further fundamental distinction was made between fixed-satellite services, mobile-satellite services and broadcasting-satellite services, currently the Radio Regulations for the purpose of allocation recognize no fewer than 21 specific space services amongst a total of 42 services.[246] Further distinguishing globally between three ITU regions, separating primary from secondary allocations, and allowing for footnote allocations deviating from the more general allocations, this results in a very complex system for interference-avoidance finetuned to the needs and interests of the member States and their operators.[247]

The allocation of frequency bands is determined by the collective ITU member States at the World Radio Conferences (previously World Administrative Radio Conferences), which usually take place every three or four years. The result of such allocations is laid down in the Table of Frequency Allocations, incorporated in the Radio Regulations.[248] The Table of Frequency Allocations itself encompasses all frequencies practically useful for telecommunication purposes, currently running from 8.3 kHz to 275 GHz,[249] which largely for convenience's sake have been subdivided into a large number of frequency bands bookended by specific frequencies, often summarized at a higher level with reference to two- or three-letter labels.[250]

The second step in the process of arranging the international use of the radio frequency spectrum effectively concerns 'allotment', which

---

245 See also Art. 1(16), ITU Radio Regulations (*supra* n. 243).
246 See Art. 1(19)–(60), ITU Radio Regulations (*supra* n. 243).
247 See for further details e.g. F.G. von der Dunk, Legal Aspects of Satellite Communications, in *Handbook of Space Law* (Eds. F.G. von der Dunk & F. Tronchetti) (2015), 467–72; also F. Lyall, On the Reform of the ITU and the Commercial Use of Space, in *'Project 2001' – Legal Framework for the Commercial Use of Outer Space* (Ed. K.H. Böckstiegel) (2002), 259–81; Bohlmann, Schrogl & Zilioli (*supra* n. 179), 204 ff., esp. 210–16.
248 See Art. 5.53–5.565, ITU Radio Regulations (*supra* n. 243).
249 The bands below 8.3 kHz are 'not allocated', and so are those between 275 and 3000 GHz; ITU Radio Regulations (*supra* n. 243).
250 See further on this Von der Dunk, *supra* n. 247, 470–2.

refers to the 'reservation' of specific *frequencies* to *States* for the purpose of specific telecommunication *services* intended to be provided.[251] In order to realize allotment in a manner not interfering with other lawful international usage of the frequency spectrum within the ITU framework, each time such interference-free access to a frequency or set of frequencies was requested by a State an extended coordination process entered into operation, essentially allowing other States with prior rights to protest if they expected harmful interference to result from the proposed newcomer. Ultimately, a frequency or set of frequencies was to be arrived at not giving rise to *any* such concerns (as long as valid).

If indeed the radio frequencies thus allotted were to be used by the State concerned itself, the step of 'assignment' properly speaking would automatically follow: 'assignment' concerns the 'reservation' of specific *frequencies* to specific *operators* for purposes of the services these intended to provide – many of the clauses discussed above with respect to allotment actually (also) already refer to assignment.[252]

If, in contrast, the actual intended operator would either be an intergovernmental organization or a private operator, neither of those having independent competence to formally request the 'allotment' of frequencies, 'assignment' would effectively constitute a distinct third step whereby the State to which the frequencies were allotted would formally permit that operator to use them. In the case of an intergovernmental organization, that would normally be the host State of that organization; in the case of a private operator, essentially in line with Article VI of the Outer Space Treaty[253] it would usually be the State under whose (territorial) jurisdiction that operator falls. Once thus assigned, the frequencies in question would by way of a Notification Request be included in the Master International Frequency Register, and by that token would be legally protected against interference by others.[254]

Given that the use of radio frequencies without interference was essentially required for all space activities, and that the ITU, in existence by then for almost a century, had quickly – and with the consent of all

---

251 See Art. 1(17), ITU Radio Regulations (*supra* n. 243).
252 See Art. 1(18), ITU Radio Regulations (*supra* n. 243).
253 See *supra*, § 1.2.
254 See also Von der Dunk, *supra* n. 247, 474–5.

relevant States concerned – picked up the task of coordinating interference-free usage also of space frequencies, the discussion of which regime should, as *lex specialis* or perhaps *lex posterior*, be deemed to have priority in case of conflicts or incompatibilities, was effectively avoided: the core body of space law developed in the bosom of the United Nations, notably its Committee on the Peaceful Uses of Outer Space, simply sought to avoid any interference in the legal field with ITU's work itself.

None of the four core outer space treaties touched upon the issue of frequency and orbital usage as addressed under the ITU regime, and it may be understood that the reference in the Outer Space Treaty to 'carry on activities in the exploration and use of outer space (...) in accordance with international law'[255] included that part of international law which, as per that same ITU regime, essentially already since 1959 had addressed the usage of frequencies and orbits.

Ever since, rather than getting into each other's hair in further developing international space law, the two organizations diligently coordinated their respective activities. The member States of ITU limited the continuing development of regulation in that context to the operational and technical aspects of the use of radio waves, including coordination of the use of relevant orbits, whereas the member States of COPUOS discussed all other aspects of space objects, including if used for telecommunications. Even when topics overlapped, such as with discussions on the mitigation of space debris,[256] the intensive coordination between the two organizations has so far succeeded in avoiding or working around any substantial conflicts or incompatibilities.[257]

4.3 International law on military activities and operations in space

Different from international telecommunications law, the legal aspects of military activities and operations, in particular the threat or use of armed force, were not avoided altogether in the space treaties –

---

255 Art. III, Outer Space Treaty (*supra* n. 4).
256 See further *supra*, § 2.6.
257 See further *e.g.* J.F. Mayence, Harmful Interference in Telecommunications under International and National Space Law, in *Harmful Interference in Regulatory Perspective* (Ed. M. Hofmann) (2015), 102–6.

logically, in view of the major rationale behind, and focus of, in particular the Outer Space Treaty in terms of addressing concerns that international peace and security might be at risk in the context of the space race. As addressed above, Articles IV, X and XI of the Outer Space Treaty already provided for a few baseline rules having a major impact in the context of military uses of this particular realm.[258]

At the same time, Article III of the Outer Space Treaty itself already made clear that the legal regime applicable to military uses of outer space was not confined to what the Outer Space Treaty itself (or any follow-up space treaty for that matter) provided; the major reason for this Article, given the specific references to the UN Charter and 'the interest of maintaining international peace and security', was to ensure that general international rules aiming to limit or even eliminate any threats to such international peace and security would, as much as possible and where relevant, apply in outer space as well.

The key question then becomes: to what extent was such insertion indeed 'possible and relevant'? In other words: if the international legal regime addressing the threat and use of force and other military issues on Earth was to be seen as a *lex specialis* with respect to the *lex generalis* of general international law, since it would supersede, suspend or even cancel otherwise applicable rules of the latter in specifically circumscribed contexts of use of armed force or other military activities as per the former, would it thereby also have priority over that other *lex specialis* of outer space law?

This is a rather complex question, as 'terrestrial' international law on military activities and operations, including the threat or use of armed force as the most salient and dangerous element thereof, had evolved over a long time and along many different paths and sometimes did, but often did not, somehow include outer space in its scope as well.

This even included one treaty that was so crucial to space that some authors actually considered it a core part of the *corpus iuris spatialis internationalis*: the 1963 Partial Test Ban Treaty.[259] Famously, it prohibited 'any nuclear weapon test explosion, or any other nuclear explosion, at any place under its jurisdiction or control: (a) in the atmosphere;

---

258 See *supra*, § 2.2.
259 *Supra*, n. 38. See further S. Kadelbach, Nuclear Weapons and Warfare, in *The Max Planck Encyclopedia of Public International Law* (Ed. R. Wolfrum) *Vol. VII* (2012), 878.

beyond its limits, including outer space'.²⁶⁰ Ratified currently by 126 States and signed by 10 more,²⁶¹ the most important States missing from the perspective of (military) nuclear capabilities, China and France, have been seen as silently acknowledging the need to abstain from such explosions in outer space, whereas North Korea is considered not yet capable of undertaking such explosions in a controlled manner so as to provide it with relevant direct military capabilities.²⁶²

Efforts to move the ban on nuclear explosions, in particular the testing of nuclear weapons, to an absolute level by way of the 1996 Comprehensive Test Ban Treaty²⁶³ have so far failed to materialize, at least as far as that treaty is concerned: although carrying 168 ratifications and 16 further signatories, eight ratifications of specific States needed for the treaty to enter into force are missing.²⁶⁴

Another treaty established along similar lines with relevance for outer space and military uses thereof concerns the 1977 ENMOD Convention,²⁶⁵ which prohibits the deliberate manipulation of the environment and natural processes for military purposes, which environment as per Article II includes outer space.²⁶⁶ Currently the treaty has 78 States parties, plus 16 signatories;²⁶⁷ among the former are the United States, China, Russia, India and most major Western European States – France is probably the most important State missing from the list.

Those treaties constitute the main examples, at least as relevant for outer space, of multilateral treaties having more or less global scope addressing specifics of military operations and activities, including the use or threat of armed force. A more informal and not legally binding

---

260 Art. I(1), Partial Test Ban Treaty (*supra* n. 38).
261 See https://en.wikipedia.org/wiki/Partial_Nuclear_Test_Ban_Treaty (last accessed 16 June 2020).
262 *Cf.* further also Tronchetti, *supra* n. 62, 343–4.
263 Comprehensive Test Ban Treaty, New York, done 24 September 1996, not yet entered into force; Cm. 3665; S. Treaty Doc. No. 105-28 (1997); 35 ILM 1439 (1996).
264 See https://en.wikipedia.org/wiki/Comprehensive_Nuclear-Test-Ban_Treaty (last accessed 16 June 2020). The eight States are China, Egypt, India, Iran, Israel, North Korea, Pakistan and the United States.
265 Convention on the Prohibition of Military and Other Hostile Use of Environmental Modification Techniques, Geneva, done 18 May 1977, entered into force 5 October 1978; 1108 UNTS 151; TIAS 9614; 31 UST 333; UKTS 1979 No. 24; Cmnd. 6985; ATS 1984 No. 22; 16 ILM 88 (1977).
266 See Tronchetti, *supra* n. 62, 344–5.
267 See https://en.wikipedia.org/wiki/Environmental_Modification_Convention (last accessed 16 June 2020).

document along the same lines is the International Code of Conduct against Ballistic Missile Proliferation.[268] The purpose of the ICOC is to stop ballistic missile proliferation: States committed to not supporting ballistic missile programmes in other States suspected of developing nuclear, biological or chemical weapons, should exercise the necessary vigilance in assisting foreign space launch programmes, and should establish transparency and confidence-building measures by requiring the exchange of pre-launch notifications on any relevant launches.[269]

None of the above would present serious risks of potential conflict or incompatibility with the inner core of the *corpus iuris spatialis internationalis*. On the contrary, in most respects they reinforce and detail such general obligations under the Outer Space Treaty as pertaining to 'the interest of maintaining international peace and security',[270] 'exclusively peaceful purposes'[271] and the need to avoid harmful interference with legitimate space activities of others.[272]

Given the preponderance in space of the two superpowers in the early decades of the Space Age, in particular in the military realm, a series of bilateral agreements on arms controls between the United States and the Soviet Union were concluded that also had some relevance in the present context. Most notably, as long as it lasted the 1972 ABM Treaty[273] as further augmented by a 1974 Protocol[274] banned the testing and deployment of anti-satellite weapons in space[275] and required of each State 'not to interfere with the national technical means of verification of the other Party',[276] which 'national technical means of

---

268 International Code of Conduct against Ballistic Missile Proliferation (hereafter ICOC), The Hague, 25 November 2002. Currently it has 138 signatories; see https://en.wikipedia.org/wiki/International_Code_of_Conduct_against_Ballistic_Missile_Proliferation (last accessed 16 June 2020).
269 See Tronchetti, *supra* n. 62, 346–7.
270 Art. III, Outer Space Treaty (*supra* n. 4).
271 Art. IV, Outer Space Treaty (*supra* n. 4).
272 *Cf.* Art. IX, Outer Space Treaty (*supra* n. 4).
273 Treaty Between the United States of America and the Union of Socialist Soviet Republics on the Limitation of Anti-Ballistic Missile Systems (hereafter ABM Treaty), Moscow, done 26 May 1972, entered into force 3 October 1972, no longer in effect 13 June 2002; 944 UNTS 13; TIAS 7503; 23 UST 3435.
274 Protocol to the Treaty Between the United States of America and the Union of Soviet Socialist Republics on the Limitation of Anti-Ballistic Missile Systems, Moscow, done 3 July 1974, entered into force 24 May 1976; TIAS 8276; 27 UST 1645.
275 See Art. V, ABM Treaty (*supra* n. 273).
276 Art. XII(2), ABM Treaty (*supra* n. 273).

verification' were specifically inclusive of remote sensing satellites, thereby acknowledging the principal right to use satellites for verification purposes.[277]

Also in this context a potential for conflicting interference with the *corpus iuris spatialis internationalis* did not arise; both States voluntarily limited their military presence and possibilities in outer space beyond the baseline limitations to those that had already been imposed by their partisanship to the Outer Space Treaty.

Those problems of potential incompatibility, in contrast, *did* arise to some extent when it came to the large body of law that originally was considered to comprise the *ius ad bellum* and the *ius in bello*, and has meanwhile come to be known more generally as the law of armed conflict.

The parts which used to be known as the *ius in bello*, also now labelled 'international humanitarian law', very much focused on efforts to protect human dignity, safety and security in the context of armed conflicts as much as possible.[278]

This was done on the one hand by what is known as the 'Geneva system', originating from the involvement of the Red Cross in the second half of the nineteenth century in efforts to alleviate human suffering on battlefields and then broader in the context of armed conflicts, such as with respect to treatment of prisoners of war.[279] Until,

---

277 See further Tronchetti, *supra* n. 62, 347–8.
278 See also already, as targeting the application in outer space, Tronchetti, *supra* n. 62, 357–9.
279 The Geneva system comprises the four Geneva Conventions (Geneva Convention for the Amelioration of the Condition of the Wounded and Sick in Armed Forces in the Field, Geneva, done 12 August 1949, entered into force 21 October 1950; 75 UNTS 31; TIAS No. 3362; 6 UST 3114; ATS 1958 No. 21; Geneva Convention for the Amelioration of the Condition of the Wounded, Sick and Shipwrecked Members of Armed Forces at Sea, Geneva, done 12 August 1949, entered into force 21 October 1950; 75 UNTS 85; TIAS No. 3363; 6 UST 3217; ATS 1958 No. 21; Geneva Convention relative to the Treatment of Prisoners of War, Geneva, done 12 August 1949, entered into force 21 October 1950; 75 UNTS 135; TIAS No. 3364; 6 UST 3316; ATS 1958 No. 21; and Geneva Convention relative to the Protection of Civilian Persons in Time of War, Geneva, done 12 August 1949, entered into force 21 October 1950; 75 UNTS 287; TIAS No. 3365; 6 UST 3516; ATS 1958 No. 21) and three Additional Protocols (Protocol Additional to the Geneva Conventions of 12 August 1949, and relating to the Protection of Victims of International Armed Conflicts, Geneva, done 8 June 1977, entered into force 7 December 1978; 1125 UNTS 3; UKTS 1999 No. 29; Cm. 4338; ATS 1991 No. 29; 16 ILM 1391 (1977); 72 AJIL 457 (1978); Protocol Additional to the Geneva Conventions of 12 August 1949, and relating to the Protection of Victims of Non-International Armed Conflicts, Geneva, done 8 June 1977, entered into force 7 December 1978; UKTS 1999 No. 30; Cm. 4339; ATS 1991 No. 30; 16 ILM 1442 (1977); 72 AJIL 502 (1978); and Protocol Additional

however, 'battlefields' are actually situated in outer space *and* humans are 'on' them, thereby becoming subjected to the possibility of being wounded or being taken prisoner, the potential for any incompatibility between the Geneva system and the *corpus iuris spatialis internationalis* remains a rather theoretical issue, whereas for battlefields on Earth any involvement of space technology does not fundamentally challenge or even change the application of the former.

On the other hand, the 'Hague system', originating in the Hague Peace Conferences of 1899 and 1907, broadened the focus beyond the Geneva system by also addressing such issues as the rights of civilians and neutral States in the context of an armed conflict and the need to strive for disarmament and peaceful settlement of disputes.[280] Thus, the 1907 Peace Conference *inter alia* gave rise to the Convention relative to the Rights and Duties of Neutral Powers and Persons in Case of War on Land[281] and the Convention concerning the Rights and Duties of Neutral Powers in Naval War.[282]

---

to the Geneva Conventions of 12 August 1949, and relating to the Adoption of an Additional Distinctive Emblem, Geneva, done 8 December 2005, entered into force 14 January 2007; Cm. 6917; S. Treaty Doc. No. 109-10 (2006); 2005 WL 4701955). The four Conventions and three Protocols are almost universally ratified (the conventions count 196 States parties; see https://en.wikipedia.org/wiki/Geneva_Conventions (last accessed 16 June 2020), the protocols respectively 174 (see https://en.wikipedia.org/wiki/Protocol_I; last accessed 16 June 2020), 169 (see https://en.wikipedia.org/wiki/Additional_Protocol_II; last accessed 16 June 2020) and 76 (see https://en.wikipedia.org/wiki/Protocol_III; last accessed 16 June 2020)), and (especially the Conventions) are by and large considered to reflect customary international law; see H.P. Gasser & D. Thürer, Geneva Conventions I–IV (1949), in *The Max Planck Encyclopedia of Public International Law* (Ed. R. Wolfrum) *Vol. IV* (2012), 386–96; E. Crawford, Geneva Conventions Additional Protocol I (1977), in *The Max Planck Encyclopedia of Public International Law* (Ed. R. Wolfrum) *Vol. IV* (2012), 396–401; E. Crawford, Geneva Conventions Additional Protocol II (1977), in *The Max Planck Encyclopedia of Public International Law* (Ed. R. Wolfrum) *Vol. IV* (2012), 401–5.

280 The Hague system comprises three Conventions resulting from the 1899 Peace Conference and 13 resulting from the 1907 one, plus attendant Declarations and Regulations, many of them widely ratified as well as otherwise of major impact on the development of the *ius in bello* and *ius ad bellum*; see B. Baker, Hague Peace Conferences (1899 and 1907), in *The Max Planck Encyclopedia of Public International Law* (Ed. R. Wolfrum) *Vol. IV* (2012), 689–98; also https://en.wikipedia.org/wiki/Hague_Conventions_of_1899_and_1907 (last accessed 16 June 2020).

281 Convention respecting the Rights and Duties of Neutral Powers and Persons in Case of War on Land; The Hague, done 18 October 1907, entered into force 26 January 1910; 36 Stat. 2310; 1 Bevans 654; D. Schindler & J. Toman, *The Laws of Armed Conflicts* (1988), 942–7. The Convention currently has 34 States parties and 17 States signatories; see https://ihl-databases.icrc.org/ihl/INTRO/200?OpenDocument (last accessed 16 June 2020).

282 Convention concerning the Rights and Duties of Neutral Powers in Naval War; The Hague, done 18 October 1907, entered into force 26 January 1910; 36 Stat. 2415; Treaty Series 545; D. Schindler & J. Toman, *The Laws of Armed Conflicts* (1988), 951–7. The Convention

By doing so, the Hague system actually also addressed some of the major issues involved in the *ius ad bellum*: under what circumstances and subject to which conditions is the use of armed force by one State in the context of a conflict with another legitimate? Following two devastating World Wars and an increasing focus on efforts to get international conflicts settled by peaceful or even juridical means,[283] this *ius ad bellum* effectively culminated in the establishment of the UN Charter and the United Nations as the premier international instrument for minimizing the use of armed force in inter-State conflicts and mitigating its dire consequences wherever armed force still came to be used.

The cornerstone of the current law of armed conflict therefore, other than the international humanitarian law stemming from the Geneva and Hague systems which continued to be enhanced and developed also under UN auspices, is formed by the fundamental provisions that all UN member States 'settle their international disputes by peaceful means in such a manner that international peace and security, and justice, are not endangered'[284] and 'shall refrain in their international relations from the threat or use of force against the territorial integrity or political independence of any state, or in any other manner inconsistent with the Purposes of the United Nations'.[285]

Given the Second World War background to the UN Charter, the reference to 'force against the territorial integrity or political independence', read against a State's sovereign existence, was understood indeed to refer to *armed* force, massive troops and armaments invading or threatening to invade another country. Consequently, only two major exceptions to the prohibition on such use of armed force against a(nother) State's sovereignty could be accepted, at least as far as the Charter itself was concerned:[286] the right of self-defence, individually or collectively, against such an armed attack[287] and the right of collective

---

currently has 30 States parties and 18 States signatories; see https://ihl-databases.icrc.org/ihl/INTRO/240?OpenDocument (last accessed 16 June 2020).
283 *Cf.* already Art. 1, also Preamble, UN Charter (*supra* n. 37).
284 Art. 2(3), UN Charter (*supra* n. 37).
285 Art. 2(4), UN Charter (*supra* n. 37).
286 Since in particular the right of self-defence was framed as an 'inherent right', meaning it existed outside of the Charter, discussions continue to rage as to whether that inherent right might be broader than the one formulated in the Charter and include *e.g.* anticipatory self-defence. See further *e.g.* in great detail Crawford, *supra* n. 21, 746–74.
287 Art. 51, UN Charter (*supra* n. 37).

action ordained by the UN Security Council involving 'air, sea, or land forces as may be necessary to maintain or restore international peace and security. Such action may include demonstrations, blockades, and other operations by air, sea, or land forces of Members of the United Nations'.[288]

Whereas later interpretations sought to broaden the reference to the threat or use of force against the territorial integrity and political independence of a State to include *economic* force or other more indirect means of posing threats to a State's sovereign existence, in the context of outer space these terms came to be subject to a rather different discussion.[289]

Would the use of force against a State's satellite in particular, be equivalent to the use of force against 'the territorial integrity or political independence' of that State, so as to trigger the right of self-defence possibly legitimizing the use of retaliatory force against space-based alternatively terrestrial counter-targets? And what if the 'force' was not the classical kinetic force destroying its target in a clearly visible physical sense, but consisted of the use of cyber technology to achieve a *de facto* equally crippling result? What if the targeted satellite was not only a satellite used for military purposes by the 'enemy State', but also for civil, perhaps even humanitarian purposes, by that same State, or its private citizens or companies, or even by third States – a situation in outer space not all that uncommon in view of the major extent of international cooperation?[290]

While these questions are already difficult enough as they are – they are currently being addressed in the context of the Woomera Manual project, which is drafting the Woomera Manual on the International Law of Military Space Operations[291] – an even more fundamental issue underlying many of the above problems concerns, as already alluded to, whether the law of armed conflict developed as discussed here, a *lex specialis* to the *lex generalis* of general international law, overrides the *corpus iuris spatialis internationalis* as *another lex specialis* to the *lex*

---

288 Art. 42, UN Charter (*supra* n. 37).
289 See further for an extended analysis R.A. Ramey, Armed Conflict on the Final Frontier: The Law of War in Space, 48 *Air Force Law Review* (2000), 1–158.
290 See further *e.g.* E.S. Waldrop, Integration of Military and Civilian Space Assets: Legal and National Security Implications, 55 *Air Force Law Review* (2004), 157–231.
291 See further https://law.adelaide.edu.au/woomera/home (last accessed 16 June 2020).

generalis of general international law, or whether it would rather be the other way around.

The law of armed conflict, while trying to impose certain limits on what is legitimate and legal in the context of an armed conflict, of course builds on the assumption that in a number of cases (armed) force will be used and may indeed even be used legally. At the same time, however, as discussed, the Outer Space Treaty prohibits the orbiting or stationing of weapons of mass destruction in outer space as well as anything but exclusively peaceful activities on the Moon and other celestial bodies[292] and generally calls for space activities to be in the interest of humankind and promote international peace and security;[293] the Rescue Agreement requires any astronaut from another country (without excepting those of the opponent in an armed conflict) to be immediately and safely repatriated;[294] the Liability Convention requires States to compensate for damage caused by space objects launched by them (without excepting as such damage caused on purpose to an opponent as part of a military campaign);[295] the Registration Convention requires every space object launched to be registered (in principle even if it is a military satellite loaded with weapons);[296] and developing customary international law on space debris would consider wanton destruction of space objects out of order (in principle also if in the context of an armed conflict).[297]

The various scenarios in the context of armed conflicts involving space that are bracketed above clearly highlight the need for prioritization. However, neither treaty law nor customary international law provide direct clues on how to solve such a prioritization of one regime of *lex specialis* over another: treaties on the law of armed conflict seldom refer directly to space assets whereas treaties on space law presume, for better or worse, the absence of armed conflict in outer space, and – fortunately of course – we have no real State practice on armed conflicts in outer space allowing us more than a glimpse of *opinio iuris*.

---

292 See Art. IV, Outer Space Treaty (*supra* n. 4); further *supra*, § 2.2.
293 See Arts. I, III, Outer Space Treaty (*supra* n. 4); further *supra*, § 2.2.
294 See Art. 4, Rescue Agreement (*supra* n. 30); further *supra*, § 2.3.
295 See Arts. I–V, Liability Convention (*supra* n. 15); further *supra*, § 2.4.
296 See Arts. I–IV, Registration Convention (*supra* n. 17); further *supra*, § 2.5.
297 See *supra*, § 2.6.

At the highest level, nevertheless, the conundrum is relatively easily solved. On the one hand, logically speaking the law of armed conflict should – subject to the conditions and parameters it itself imposes, such as on targeting, proportionality, military necessity and suchlike[298] – override outer space law wherever the two would conflict or be incompatible. It would be difficult to imagine that States would really have understood for instance the Liability Convention to require the payment of compensation also for any damage caused to an 'enemy' by means of a space object and would have ratified any such treaty on the basis of such an assumption. Or to assume that even in the context of self-defence or other justified use of armed force military operations on the Moon would be prohibited by the Outer Space Treaty.

This approach is, moreover, borne out by the UN Charter itself, which on the one hand posits the most fundamental premises on which the law of armed conflict is built, that is self-defence and the Security Council's powers to wage war on a State threatening international peace and security,[299] and on the other hand declares: 'In the event of a conflict between the obligations of the Members of the United Nations under the present Charter and their obligations under any other international agreement, their obligations under the present Charter shall prevail'.[300] This raises the fundamental tenets of the law of armed conflict as based on the Charter to a higher hierarchical status than the law of outer space as based on the Outer Space Treaty and its follow-up treaties.

On the other hand, that should not be taken to mean that the *corpus iuris spatialis internationalis* is bereft of any legal significance as soon as an armed conflict occurs, that it would be a mere paper effort to stave off such armed conflicts which is ultimately without power and meaning if an armed conflict would nevertheless arise.

The key here is the distinction that has to be made between the legal relation between the parties to the armed conflict on the one hand and the legal relation between any of those and third parties on the other. In other words, the law of armed conflict supersedes obligations under international space law *only* as between the belligerents (and then, furthermore, as said only in as far as its own conditions and

---

298 See *e.g.* Ramey, *supra* n. 289, 34–44.
299 As per Arts. 51 & 42, UN Charter (*supra* n. 37); see further Tronchetti, *supra* n. 62, 350–6.
300 Art. 103, UN Charter (*supra* n. 37).

parameters allow for), but *vis-à-vis* all other States and their entities, which should effectively be treated as neutrals to the conflict (again, as per the parameters and conditions that the law of armed conflict has developed to determine neutral and other non-belligerent status[301]), the *corpus* maintains its full legal application.

Given the intricate complex international relations and cooperation mechanisms in terms of space activities, at the second level it then yet remains to be determined how to assess and address the various scenarios that may arise, whereby a particular space operation or space object may have both 'enemy' and 'neutral' aspects and elements and the relative value of either needs to be determined in order to allow for a proper evaluation as a military target from the perspective of proportionality and military necessity,[302] or whether for instance the obligation towards third States *not* to orbit weapons of mass destruction would override or limit any right to use weapons of mass destruction in case the naked survival of a State is considered to be at stake – or the other way around.

A final development that merits being addressed here concerns the efforts led by Russia and China to generate support for a Draft Treaty on the Prevention of the Placement of Weapons in Outer Space, the Threat or Use of Force against Outer Space Objects (PPWT) presented in 2008.[303] Its main weaknesses, which have so far prevented it from generating much interest in ratifying it, concern the problem of sensibly and accurately defining a weapon in a context where *any* object could be used as a weapon in view of the velocity of movement, the ignorance of the legitimacy of using armed force in self-defence or in the context of UN-mandated military actions which would also apply in principle to outer space, and the ignorance of more pressing threats to the safety and security of any space operations caused by space debris.[304]

---

301 Note, however, that even the two Hague Conventions directly and comprehensively addressing 'neutrality' in their respective domains (*supra* ns. 281 & 282) have refrained from defining 'neutral State' or 'neutral Power'.

302 *Cf. e.g.* for a major effort at analysis W.H. von Heinegg, Neutrality and Outer Space, 93 *International Law Studies* (2017), 526–47.

303 Draft Treaty on the Prevention of the Placement of Weapons in Outer Space, the Threat or Use of Force against Outer Space Objects (hereafter Draft PPWT); UN Doc. CD/1985, 12 June 2014; http://www.reachingcriticalwill.org/images/documents/Disarmament-fora/cd/2014/documents/PPWT2014.pdf (last accessed 16 June 2020).

304 See further Tronchetti, *supra* n. 62, 378–9; F.G. von der Dunk, Cutting the Bread, 29 *Space Policy* (2013), 231–3.

To try and remedy those flaws, focusing more on the aggressive military use of any space asset than on the hardware itself and taking space debris explicitly in its stride, a Draft International Code of Conduct for Outer Space Activities was proposed by the European Union also in 2008.[305] While the Code, even though essentially qualifying as soft law with the mere hope of future evolution into customary international law, also failed for ulterior reasons, because of the different focus of its substance it makes considerably more sense than the Draft PPWT – and thereby might still, at some point in the future, present the point of departure for development into such a customary international law regime.[306]

4.4 The international regimes addressing sensitive dual-use space technologies

Almost all space activities by definition have, if not actual implications in the military and security realm, at least potentially serious consequences in that context – and hence would qualify as involving dual-use technologies, likely moreover often of a sensitive nature. The difference between a launch vehicle and a missile is often marginal; satellites can be used for perfectly peaceful operations but also to purposefully collide with other satellites; satellite navigation can guide cars and mountaineers as well as tanks and missiles; and satellite remote sensing data can show environmental degradation as much as the build-up of armaments.

Logically, therefore, in particular States possessing the most advanced technologies in those realms are keen on controlling the trafficking of such technologies to prevent them from ending up in the hands of potential or actual adversaries – and in doing so, posing major obstacles to civil, peaceful and/or commercial space operations and services.

On the one hand, this has given rise to a handful of international regimes whereby like-minded States undertook an effort to control

---

305 International Code of Conduct for Outer Space Activities; http://www.eeas.europa.eu/non-proliferation-and-disarmament/pdf/space_code_conduct_draft_vers_31-march-2014_en.pdf (last accessed 16 June 2020).
306 See further W. Rathgeber, N.L. Remuss & K.U. Schrogl, Space Security and the European Code of Conduct for Outer Space Activities, 4 *Disarmament Forum* (2009), 34–41; Tronchetti, *supra* n. 62, 379–81.

such potentially threatening international technology transfers. Since the 1968 Non-Proliferation Treaty[307] had not formally included in the prohibition of proliferation of nuclear *weapons* the possible delivery mechanisms thereof, read bomb-carrying missiles, the Missile Technology Control Regime (MTCR)[308] was established to fill that gap.[309]

It thus focuses on rockets, and hence almost automatically has an impact on launch vehicles for peaceful, civil and commercial missions and their payloads as well. The MTCR, however, is an informal and voluntary association of, as of today, 35 participating States[310] sharing the goal of non-proliferation and willingness to coordinate national missile technology export licensing to that end – but not to accept or impose any *legal* obligations relative to granting licences or sanctions in case of export licences actually being granted.

The MTCR Guidelines for Sensitive Missile-relevant Transfers[311] form the cornerstone of the MTCR, offering a set of common export policy guidelines applied to an integral common list of controlled items: the MTCR Equipment, Software, and Technology Annex.[312] Decisions on the guidelines and the contents of the lists are taken by consensus in order to enhance adherence, and partner States regularly exchange information about relevant national export licensing issues. As a result, many States, not just the MTCR partners, have indeed introduced export-licensing measures on such items as rockets and other delivery systems, and related equipment, material and technology.

The second major international arrangement concerned the 1995 Wassenaar Arrangement.[313] It currently counts 42 participating

---

307 Treaty on the Non-Proliferation of Nuclear Weapons, London/Moscow/Washington, done 1 July 1968, entered into force 5 March 1970; 729 UNTS 161; TIAS 6839; 21 UST 483; UKTS 1970 No. 88; Cmnd. 3683; ATS 1973 No. 3; 7 ILM 809 (1968).
308 Agreement on Guidelines for the Transfer of Equipment and Technology Related to Missiles (hereafter MTCR), done 16 April 1987; 26 ILM 599 (1987).
309 See Tronchetti, *supra* n. 62, 360–3; P. van Fenema, Legal Aspects of Launch Services and Space Transportation, in *Handbook of Space Law* (Eds. F.G. von der Dunk & F. Tronchetti) (2015), 418–20; Waldrop, *supra* n. 290, 189–90.
310 See https://en.wikipedia.org/wiki/Missile_Technology_Control_Regime (last accessed 16 June 2020).
311 See https://mtcr.info/mtcr-guidelines/ (last accessed 16 June 2020).
312 See https://mtcr.info/mtcr-annex/ (last accessed 16 June 2020).
313 Wassenaar Arrangement on Export Controls for Conventional Arms and Dual-use Goods and Technologies (hereafter Wassenaar Arrangement), Wassenaar, done 19 December 1995, effective 12 July 1996; http://www.wassenaar.org/ (last accessed 16 June 2020).

states,³¹⁴ largely the same as those participating in the MTCR. Like the MTCR, the Wassenaar Arrangement is a global, formally non-binding arrangement on export controls, except broader in scope as it applies to conventional weapons more generally as well as to, basically, any sensitive dual-use goods and technologies.

Thus, participating States commit themselves to ensuring through national policies and, where appropriate, regulations that crossborder transfers of these items do not contribute to the development or enhancement of military capabilities of certain States considered a potential threat to international security and stability.³¹⁵ As with the MTCR, under the Wassenaar Arrangement the decision to allow or deny transfer of any item remains the sole responsibility of each individual State.³¹⁶

Consequently, export controls continue to differ from country to country. The participating States only agree to *notify* transfers and denials of, as well as more generally to control export of, all items in the List of Dual-Use Goods and Technologies and the List of Munitions, annexed to the Arrangement.³¹⁷ In any event, 'controls do not apply to "technology" [including software] in the public domain [to] "basic scientific research" or to the minimum necessary information for patent applications'.³¹⁸ The List has two annexes of sensitive, respectively very sensitive items, to which different levels of control should be applied, and reviewed regularly to reflect new developments in the realm of technology. Finally, the participating States agree to exchange general information on risks associated with transfers of conventional arms and dual-use goods and technologies in order to consider, where necessary, the scope for coordinating national control policies to combat these risks.³¹⁹

Partly owing to the fundamental lack of binding force of those two international arrangements, the most important States in addition all have their own national, legally binding export control and licensing regimes, which in terms of substance largely follow the MTCR and

---

314   See https://en.wikipedia.org/wiki/Wassenaar_Arrangement (last accessed 16 June 2020).
315   See Art. I(1), Wassenaar Arrangement (*supra* n. 313).
316   See Art. II(3), Wassenaar Arrangement (*supra* n. 313).
317   As per Arts. II(4), III(1), Wassenaar Arrangement (*supra* n. 313), & Appendix 5.
318   Wassenaar Arrangement (*supra* n. 313), Dual-use List, General Technology Note, 3.
319   See Art. IV(1), Wassenaar Arrangement (*supra* n. 313).

Wassenaar Lists but maintain ultimate individual sovereignty over the decision to allow export in every individual case.

Most notably (or notoriously, as some would have it), in the United States the existing technology export controls regime started to have a serious impact on the commercial space sector as soon as the latter started to move fundamentally beyond the status of manufacturing subcontractor *vis-à-vis* the US government and the National Aeronautics and Space Administration (NASA).[320] Consequently, launch systems also capable of delivering weapons, including those of mass destruction, to terrestrial targets, and all components and key technologies involved were now included in the US Munitions List (USML),[321] which under the Arms Export Control Act[322] was subject to the jurisdiction of the US Department of State. Implementing International Traffic in Arms Regulations (ITARs) then controlled the export of such systems, components and technologies to anywhere outside the United States where their presence might result in security threats.[323]

Thus, Chapter IV of the USML comprised *inter alia*:

> (a) Rockets (including but not limited to meteorological and other sounding rockets) (...) as well as launchers for such defense articles (...)
> (b) Launch vehicles and missile and anti-missile systems including but not limited to guided, tactical and strategic missiles, launchers, and systems (...)
> (h) All specifically designed or modified components, parts, accessories, attachments, and associated equipment for the articles in this category (...)
> (i) Technical data (...) and defense services (...) directly related to the defense articles enumerated in paragraphs (a) through (h) of this category.[324]

Inclusion in such a list was perhaps less obvious with regard to satellites, even as there could be little doubt that satellites were already

---

320 See *e.g.* M.N. Gold, Lost in Space: A Practitioner's First-Hand Perspective on Reforming the U.S.'s Obsolete, Arrogant, and Counterproductive Export Control Regime for Space-Related Systems and Technologies, 34 *Journal of Space Law* (2008), 165; C. Kohlhase & P.S. Makiol, Report of the 'Project 2001' Working Group on Launch and Associated Services, in *'Project 2001' – Legal Framework for the Commercial Use of Outer Space* (Ed. K.H. Böckstiegel) (2002), 81–3.
321 United States Munitions List (USML), 22 C.F.R. 121.
322 Arms Export Control Act of 1976, 22 U.S.C. 2751.
323 See *e.g.* P.L. Meredith & S.P. Fleming, U.S. Space Technology Exports: The Current Political Climate, 27 *Journal of Space Law* (1999), 40–1.
324 USML, 22 C.F.R., § 121.1, at 469.

supporting military capabilities in many ways – examples involved the provision of intelligence, the provision of secure communications, and the guidance of missile and other weapon systems. Ever since satellite communications emerged as a viable commercial sector in the 1980s, however, the principled inclusion of satellites, their components and technologies in the USML has been beyond doubt, even if many aspects continue to be subject to debate.[325]

What made the issue even more complicated in terms of space activities, moreover, was the existence of a more or less parallel system as per the US Commerce Control List (CCL),[326] which falls within the jurisdiction of the US Department of Commerce. The CCL was ruled by the Export Administration Act,[327] which dealt with the export of dual-use items for which an export authorization was required under the Export Administration Regulations.

As long as such space items were under the control of the Department of Commerce, there was a presumption that unless direct threats to US security could be discerned, export should be allowed to boost the competitiveness of the US commercial space industry in the international arena, while the US Department of State is generally much more stringent in applying export controls.[328]

While the major European States each maintained sovereign control over their export licensing systems, the trade aspects involved and the interest of the European Union in applying its free-trade regime also to that sector gave rise to an effort to at least harmonize some aspects of national licensing systems – in a binding legal fashion.

By that token currently a 2009 Regulation,[329] updated regularly, provides for, among others, a common EU list of dual-use items along the lines of the MTCR and Wassenaar Arrangement Lists, specific control measures to be introduced by exporters and provisions setting up a

---

325 As Gold noted at the time, 'the U.S. had become the only nation that still treated commercial communication satellites as munitions'; Gold, *supra* n. 320, 165. See further Tronchetti, *supra* n. 62, 366–9; Van Fenema, *supra* n. 309, 424–5, 429–36.
326 Commerce Control List (CCL), 15 C.F.R. 774.
327 Export Administration Act of 1979, Public Law 96–72, 96th Congress, 93 Stat. 503; regularly amended since.
328 *Cf.* Van Fenema, *supra* n. 309, 429–36.
329 Council Regulation setting up a Community regime for the control of exports, transfer, brokering and transit of dual-use items, No. 428/2009/EC, of 5 May 2009; OJ L 134/1 (2009).

network of competent authorities supporting the exchange of information and the consistent implementation and enforcement of controls throughout the European Union.[330]

Most important is the introduction of the Community General Export Authorization (CGEA), which effectively constitutes a semi-automatic European-wide authorization for exports of dual-use items covered by it. The most sensitive items (such as any items involved in the development, production or handling of weapons of mass destruction), however, remain under various national controls; the requirements imposed in this regard only impose obligations related to information and consultation, wherever relevant.[331]

Still, the CGEA is an important step towards a coherent European export control regime. It deals *ratione materiae* with the bulk of items possibly requiring export controls, including those following from various sets of international obligations (from MTCR and Wassenaar Arrangement Lists to specific *ad hoc* limits imposed by international sanctions) by means of Annex I. It only allows for a relatively limited set of exceptions, following *inter alia* from Annexes II and IV. *Ratione personae*, the limitations of this harmonizing step are considerably more limited since only intra-EU trade and trade with a handful of close allies fall within the CGEA's scope.[332]

Fundamentally, the issue of dual-use security-sensitive technology export controls, as addressed in the legal and policy arena by the various international and national regimes discussed above, is purely of a terrestrial nature, wherefore the possibility of any incompatibility with the core of international space law at a practical level is fairly remote. Whatever incompatibilities might arise at some point would boil down to the sovereignty of States not as such touched upon *ratione materiae* by international space law.

It would be difficult to imagine for instance, that one would be able to successfully argue that the broad and general principles that

---

330 See https://ec.europa.eu/trade/import-and-export-rules/export-from-eu/dual-use-controls/ (last accessed 16 June 2020); further Tronchetti, *supra* n. 62, 369–77.
331 See Art. 9(1), Regulation 428/2009/EC (*supra* n. 329).
332 See also F.G. von der Dunk, A European 'Equivalent' to United States Export Controls: European Law on the Control of International Trade in Dual-Use Space Technologies, 7 *Astropolitics* (2009), 121–4.

'[o]uter space (...) shall be free for exploration and use by *all* States without discrimination of any kind, on a basis of equality' and that '[t]he exploration and use of outer space (...) shall be the province of *all* mankind'[333] overrule any sovereign right of a State to control exports of technology that could be used by a potential adversary for making use of its space freedoms and rights of access to outer space – but also could come to be used against the former's national security interests.

It is nevertheless incontrovertible that the resulting regimes exercise a major impact on the opportunities to undertake space activities and the parameters within which it would be possible to do so. In that sense, any discussion on these regimes as they impact even peaceful and commercial space activities certainly belongs in the Southern part of the first ring.

4.5 Concluding remarks

While the international telecommunications regime as applicable to outer space, the regime on the military uses of outer space and the international efforts to control the traffic in dual-use technologies are by far the most important elements of the Southern part of the first ring, many other more or less delineated international regimes would fit into this category as well.

One example concerns the issue of financing of space assets. In the 1990s, the realization dawned that with the increasing internationalization and commercialization of outer space and space activities, involving more and more start-up or non-traditional ('NewSpace') companies looking for up-front financing of their ventures, the absence of a private international law regime for asset-based financing might stand in the way of allowing NewSpace to develop properly.[334]

Consequently, UNIDROIT, the International Institute for the Unification of Private Law, took it upon itself to initiate the development

---

333 Art. I, Outer Space Treaty (*supra* n. 4); emphasis added.
334 See further M.J. Sundahl, Financing Space Ventures, in *Handbook of Space Law* (Eds. F.G. von der Dunk & F. Tronchetti) (2015), 874–909.

of a Space Assets Protocol,[335] which in combination with the framework of the Cape Town Convention[336] was to fill such a gap in the international community. 'Space assets' were defined broadly enough to encompass all objects sent into outer space as well as distinguishable, separately identifiable components, regardless of the type of space activities for which they would be intended.[337] So far, however, adherence to the Protocol has been too limited for it to even enter into force.[338] Notably, in any event potential incompatibility with the core of the *corpus iuris spatialis internationalis* was explicitly excluded: under the heading 'Relationship with the United Nations Outer Space Treaties and instruments of the International Telecommunication Union' it was provided that '[t]he Convention as applied to space assets does not affect State Party rights and obligations under the existing United Nations Outer Space Treaties or instruments of the International Telecommunication Union'.[339]

Another example of a 'niche' regime, at least from the perspective of international space law, but still potentially targeting all space activities, concerns the insurance issue.[340] While insurance includes such things as property damage insurance, this does not fundamentally relate to (international) space law: it is essentially a matter of business policy. That is different for third-party liability insurance, given the international space law regime imposing such liability upon launching States[341] and such launching States derogating through licences as desired such third-party liability to the licensee – often accompanied by an actual statutory obligation to insure against such liability.[342] Such an insurance obligation, however, by that token is very much a matter for domestic legislation rather than for an international regime, and indeed such an international regime is totally absent here.

---

335 Protocol to the Convention on International Interests in Mobile Equipment on Matters Specific to Space Assets (hereafter Space Assets Protocol), Berlin, done 9 March 2012, not yet entered into force; UNIDROIT Doc., DCME-SP-Doc. 43. See also already Reif, Schmidt-Tedd & Wannenmacher (*supra* n. 7), 441–5.
336 Convention on International Interests in Mobile Equipment, Cape Town, done 16 November 2001, entered into force 1 April 2004; ICAO Doc. 9793.
337 See further Sundahl, *supra* n. 334, 891.
338 *Cf.* also Sundahl, *supra* n. 334, 907–9.
339 Art. XXXIV, Space Assets Protocol (*supra* n. 335).
340 See further C. Gaubert, Insurance in the Context of Space Activities, in *Handbook of Space Law* (Eds. F.G. von der Dunk & F. Tronchetti) (2015), 910–48.
341 See *supra*, § 2.4.
342 See further *infra*, Von der Dunk at n. 481.

Such niche regimes as well as the others more extensively discussed in this chapter clearly are either subject to whatever relevant parameters and limitations are provided by the core of the *corpus iuris spatialis internationalis*, and to the extent applicable, the Northern part of the first ring, or apply in rather specific circumstances not really touched upon by those, confirming the basic tenet that this applies in principle to all regimes in the Southern part of the first ring. The only true exception concerns the law of armed conflict, basically as far as the UN Charter and its regime addressing international peace and security is concerned – and thereby, almost by definition, as between parties to a conflict only.

5 The second ring of space law

5.1 Introduction

As indicated, the second ring comprises those international regimes containing international law that is more or less directly relevant for only one major category of space activities, while at the same time is not particularly focused on such space activities (Figure 5.1).[343] Many experts would probably place the ITU regime in this category also, as applying to satellite communications, representing a mere category (albeit the most important, earliest and in terms of financial size by far the largest commercial sector of space applications) within space activities at large. However, as discussed, that regime actually applies to *all* uses of radio frequencies in or with respect to outer space, including TT&C functions with regard to space objects engaged in applications other than satellite communications, ranging from remote sensing to manned spaceflight; hence it has been addressed as falling within the Southern part of the first ring.[344]

The most important international law regimes in the second ring, therefore, may be deemed to be the triad of intellectual property rights in the context of space activities in view of the latter's highly expensive and technologically advanced character; the involvement of air law in the context of legislating for and regulating commercial (in particular manned) spaceflight; and the international trade regime currently relevant for satellite communication services only, as developed in the context of the WTO.

It should be caveated that strictly speaking the first and last regimes do not belong in the second ring in a straightforward manner, at least from

---

343 Again, Art. III, Outer Space Treaty (*supra* n. 4), implies that *all* international law would be part of space law in a broader sense, at least as long not incompatible or conflicting with those parts of international law that specifically address space activities as a *lex specialis*.
344 See *supra*, § 4.2.

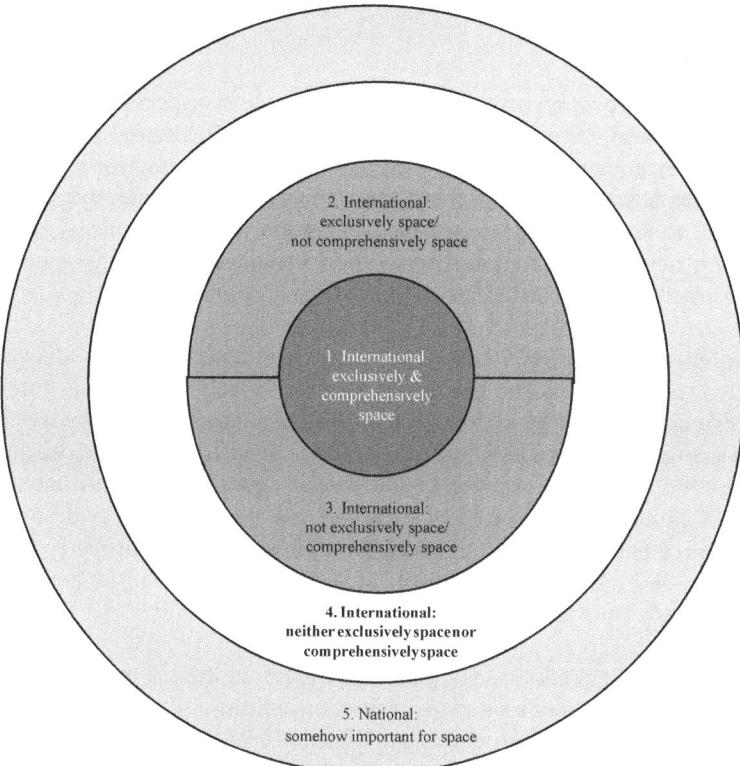

Figure 5.1 The second ring of space law

a theoretical perspective. As for intellectual property rights, in particular patent rights would be important in principle for *all* relevant technology development. In practice, however, given that most technology development takes place on Earth, the specific phenomenon of inventions *in* outer space remains fairly limited to the ISS, whereas 'space copyrights' so far are mainly an issue in the context of satellite remote sensing only. As for international trade law, the regime developed in the context of the WTO could in principle apply – and may perhaps in the future come to be applied – to a range of different space activities, but both *de iure* and *de facto* has so far been limited to satellite communications.[345]

---

345 *Cf.* also F.G. von der Dunk, International Trade Aspects of Space Services, in *Handbook of Space Law* (Eds. F.G. von der Dunk & F. Tronchetti) (2015), 836–43, 853–72, for a discussion of the potential application of the WTO regime to launch services, satellite remote sensing, satellite navigation and manned spaceflight operations – which so far largely remains theory.

5.2 Intellectual property rights in the context of space activities

Intellectual property rights is a classic example of a specific set of legal regimes and rules developed long before humans entered into outer space even by proxy, yet was next viewed with great interest by major groups of stakeholders in the space arena as offering sharp and strong legal tools to protect and/or further certain of their interests – and then nevertheless required some level of adaptation to the specific character of space activities and major space applications.

Intellectual property rights as a concept concerns the rights enjoyed by private persons and entities to own the invisible/intangible, 'intellectual' source of their work, and to protect such ownership by law.[346] Generally, such property rights have been classified into two broad and generic categories, copyrights and similar rights, respectively patents and similar rights, but all of these regimes essentially provide for a balance between the interests of the individual whose property is at stake, and the interests of society at large in being able ultimately also to benefit from such property.

Copyright regimes usually also encompass additional neighbouring rights such as those related to production, editing and publishing, photographs, computer programs and databases. The essence of copyright is that protection of the content of a certain piece of work stimulates individuals to undertake the effort of creating it in the first place; they may be sure that (at least in law) free-riding is disallowed, since creators have an exclusive right to their own work. Of course, they can then also use this right as a revenue-generating tool by allowing others against a fee to reproduce the work in copies, to prepare derivative works based on the original work and/or to distribute copies to the public for exploitation purposes.

Patent rights, as well as closely related trademarks, service marks and suchlike, operate essentially in a similar fashion to establish a balance between the interests of society in stimulating individual creativity for the benefit of the public at large and the interests of that individual in personally reaping the benefits of his creativity. Ownership of a patent

---

346 See further C. Doldirina, Intellectual Property Rights in the Context of Space Activities, in *Handbook of Space Law* (Eds. F.G. von der Dunk & F. Tronchetti) (2015), 949–94; also Reif, Schmidt-Tedd & Wannenmacher (*supra* n. 7), 434–8.

for instance, basically entitles the owner to exclusive control over the invention thus patented for many years to come, depending, of course, on something qualifying for patentability as an 'invention'. It thus provides the prospective inventor with financial benefits resulting from his invention by licensing others to use it against payment of royalties, translating patent ownership into a revenue-generating mechanism for the patent holder.

Copyright regimes have been developed on a national level since the seventeenth century,[347] patent rights already as early as the late fifteenth century.[348] Protection and enforcement of such intellectual property rights was an obvious prerogative of individual sovereign States, whose jurisdiction in those realms was essentially limited to respective national territories. Consequently, in order to achieve some measure of protection of a copyright or patent right also in other countries, it was necessary to conclude international treaties, whereby the States parties committed themselves to at least recognize copyrights or patent rights granted in other States as being entitled to protection and enforcement also on their own territories, and in the process usually also to work towards harmonization of such intellectual property rights regimes in terms of substance.

Some of these treaties belong to the earliest multilateral treaties with almost global application: the 1886 Berne Convention[349] on copyrights currently counts 177 States parties;[350] the 1883 Paris Convention[351] addressing patents and similar rights has exactly the same number of States parties.[352] Later amendments to these treaties as well as separate key treaties further enhanced the global protection of intellectual

---

347 See https://en.wikipedia.org/wiki/Copyright (last accessed 16 June 2020).
348 See https://en.wikipedia.org/wiki/Patent (last accessed 16 June 2020).
349 Berne Convention for the Protection of Literary and Artistic Works, Berne, done 9 September 1886, entered into force 5 December 1887; 828 UNTS 221; 331 UNTS 217; ATS 1901 No. 126. See further T. Cottier, Industrial Property, International Protection, in *The Max Planck Encyclopedia of Public International Law* (Ed. R. Wolfrum) *Vol. V* (2012), 160–2; F.M. Abbott, Intellectual Property, International Protection, in *The Max Planck Encyclopedia of Public International Law* (Ed. R. Wolfrum) *Vol. V* (2012), 228–33.
350 See https://en.wikipedia.org/wiki/Berne_Convention (last accessed 16 June 2020).
351 Convention for the Protection of Industrial Property as Modified by Additional Act of 14 December 1900 and Final Protocol, Paris, done 20 March 1883, entered into force 6 July 1884; 828 UNTS 305; USTS 379; UKTS 1907 No. 21; ATS 1907 No. 6. See further Cottier, *supra* n. 349, 160–2; Abbott, *supra* n. 349, 228–33.
352 See https://en.wikipedia.org/wiki/Paris_Convention_for_the_Protection_of_Industrial_Property (last accessed 16 June 2020).

property rights, notably the 1967 WIPO Convention[353] establishing the World Intellectual Property Organization (WIPO).

Once humankind entered into outer space, even if largely by proxy through remotely controlled devices, it became immediately apparent that the technological aspects of space operations were paramount. First the Cold War space race between the two superpowers, then the increasing thirst for benefitting from space technologies including more and more also the private sector, resulted in a search for legal tools to somehow protect those technologies against 'free-riders' – and intellectual property rights became the logical concept to go to.

At the same time, the existing intellectual property rights regimes, national as well as international, being developed with no consideration whatsoever for their potential use in a space context, showed considerable shortcomings from that perspective. While to a certain extent technological development was key to *all* kinds of space activities, thus perhaps suggesting international intellectual property rights law to belong to discussion of the Southern part of the first ring rather than of the second ring, when it came to actual space *activities* or their *direct products*, and options to protect those by way of intellectual property rights regimes, two main sectors were implicated only.

As for copyrights, this largely concerned satellite remote sensing, including if it was part of broader services such as those involving Geographic Information Systems (GIS). For protection of the pictures – or other databases resulting from satellite remote sensing operations – copyright seemed the obvious legal instrument, but it suffered from major flaws from that perspective.

First, there were essentially two global approaches to allowing copyright protection to apply, which in itself created a considerable measure of uncertainty in the almost by definition international environment in which satellite remote sensing was undertaken. Under the more utilitarian Anglo-American approach the level of protection is relatively low, while at the same time to qualify for copyright protection the involvement of skill and labour basically suffices – the so-called 'sweat

---

353 Convention Establishing the World Intellectual Property Organization (WIPO), Stockholm, done 14 July 1967, entered into force 26 April 1970; 828 UNTS 3; TIAS 6932; 21 UST 1749; UKTS 1970 No. 52; Cmnd. 3422; ATS 1972 No. 15; 6 ILM 782 (1967). See further Cottier, *supra* n. 349, 931–40.

of the brow'. In contrast, under the more author-minded European-continental approach some measure of creativity is required for copyright eligibility, while, once having obtained copyright protection, the authors generally enjoy more rights to the fruits of their labour.

Second, this European-continental approach raised profound issues with regard to the level of creativity inherent in the, often fully or largely automated, satellite operations generating the data to be protected. Not accidentally, it was in the European context that this conundrum eventually gave rise to a specific new piece of legislation, the European Union's 1996 Database Directive.[354] It created a *sui generis* intellectual property right for electronic databases including remote sensing databases, broadly based on copyrights protection but tailoring it to the context of databases – essentially by lowering the threshold for protection to 'sweat-of-the-brow' while adding some database-specific preconditions.[355]

As for patents, the main area where space activities as such were found to be potentially benefitting from intellectual property rights protection was manned spaceflight, where humans present in outer space (mainly as active on space stations for prolonged periods of time) could invent possibly patentable technologies or items. The main issue was that patent legislation (different from copyright law) was very much territory-based: traditionally, the State on whose territory an invention was made, regardless of what nationality the inventor had, was the State whose patent regime was applicable. However, 'territory' in the legal sense was of course absent in outer space, given the fundamental principle of Article II of the Outer Space Treaty.[356]

The solution found in practice uses the opportunities offered under Article VIII of the Outer Space Treaty to 'retain jurisdiction and control' over an object launched into outer space and subsequently registered by the State concerned. For instance, the United States has by means of the 1990 Patents in Outer Space Act[357] declared that any inventions made on board of US-registered spacecraft can be patented pursuant

---

354 Directive of the European Parliament and of the Council on the legal protection of databases (hereafter Database Directive), 96/9/EC, of 11 March 1996; OJ L 77/20 (1996).
355 See Doldirina, *supra* n. 346, 955–6; also Von der Dunk, *supra* n. 196, 249–50.
356 See further *supra*, § 1.2.
357 Patents in Outer Space Act (hereafter US Patents in Space Act), 15 November 1990, Public Law 101-580; 35 U.S.C. 10; 104 Stat. 2863.

to US patent law. While in the context of the ISS, as briefly referred to,[358] the registration of the European module by ESA was handled by a clause allowing individual ESA member States to treat the ESA module for purposes of their national intellectual property rights law as a piece of national territory, Germany and Italy have both actually extended the scope of their national intellectual property laws conformingly.[359]

In the context of patent law as well, however, global harmonization has only gone so far, in many instances leading to specific problems or uncertainties. Here as well, broadly speaking two approaches are taken to patentability, best summarized respectively as 'first-to-invent' and 'first-to-file' (with a recognized, usually governmental, patent authority). The first system is generally adhered to for instance by European countries, whereas the second is *inter alia* applicable in the United States.

In sum, using specific space law clauses such as those pertaining to quasi-territorial jurisdiction on board of registered spacecraft (such as the US Patents in Space Act) or conversely drafting space-focused legislation adding on to the general regime (such as the EU Database Directive), considerable efforts have been undertaken to maximize the use of copyrights, patents and (albeit to a much lesser extent) other forms of intellectual property rights to help promote the interests of specific categories of stakeholders in the space arena.

As a corollary, references to intellectual property rights as being (potentially) applicable to the subject matter of legal regimes focused on other issues also abound – not in the four core treaties, but in many later instances. For instance, a clause on 'copyrights and neighbouring rights' was included in the Principles on Direct Broadcasting by Satellite.[360] The ESA Convention contained its own regime on handling intellectual property rights,[361] as did the Intergovernmental Agreement on the ISS.[362]

---

358 See *supra*, § 3.2.
359 See Balsano & Wheeler, *supra* n. 164, 67–9; L.J. Smith, Legal Aspects of Commercial Utilization of the International Space Station: A German Perspective, in *The International Space Station* (Eds. F.G. von der Dunk & M.M.T.A. Brus) (2006), 153–80; V. Iavicoli, Italy and the Commercial Utilization of the International Space Station, in *The International Space Station* (Eds. F.G. von der Dunk & M.M.T.A. Brus) (2006), 181–202.
360 Princ. H, Principles on Direct Broadcasting by Satellite (*supra* n. 47).
361 *Cf.* Art. III, ESA Convention (*supra* n. 35), which provide the baseline; see further Balsano & Wheeler, *supra* n. 164, esp. 67–9, 78–86.
362 *Cf.* Art. 21, Intergovernmental Agreement on the ISS (*supra* n. 32); many details were elaborated

5.3 Air law and private manned spaceflight, including space tourism

Air law is the body of law that has developed to address (mainly) civil commercial aviation, with international air law essentially being born in 1919 with the adoption of the Paris Convention,[363] which was superseded in 1944 by the Chicago Convention,[364] still as of today providing the overarching legal framework for international aviation, trickling down in many domestic legal orders.

Space technologies and operations, certainly in the realm of transportation of humans and cargo, to a large extent developed from aviation technologies and operations, so once potential commercial applications of such technologies and operations became the subject of discussion, logically the attention turned to air law for guidance with respect to the development of relevant law and regulation, probably even transposition and adaption of air law as such, to apply to these space operations.

It bears noting, however, that the applicability of air law is basically premised on two key foundational legal concepts.

One is that of the fundamental sovereignty of States over their own airspace,[365] which allowed a State to keep out any foreign aircraft or foreign operators from its own airspace, or if admitting them, to impose any conditions it considered appropriate, whether from a security, safety or economic perspective. In this area, the main function of international air law was to agree on a multilateral basis as much as possible on standardized exceptions to the basic right of States to keep foreign aircraft and their operators out in order to allow an international aviation environment to arise and to prosper.[366]

---

in the Memoranda of Understanding and further Implementing Arrangements. *Cf.* also Balsano & Wheeler, *supra* n. 164, 64 ff.

363 Convention Relating to the Regulation of Aerial Navigation (hereafter Paris Convention), Paris, done 13 October 1919, entered into force 11 July 1922; 11 LNTS 173; UKTS 1922 No. 2; ATS 1922 No. 6.

364 See *supra*, n. 125.

365 See Art. 1, Paris Convention (*supra* n. 363); Art. 1, Chicago Convention (*supra* n. 125).

366 *Cf.* further *e.g.* L. Tomas, Air Law, in *The Max Planck Encyclopedia of Public International Law* (Ed. R. Wolfrum) *Vol. I* (2012), 233–42. In the economic context this translated into such further international treaties as the International Air Services Transit Agreement, Chicago, done 7 December 1944, entered into force 30 January 1945; 84 UNTS 389; 59 Stat. 1963; UKTS

The other is the concept of an 'aircraft'. Defined as 'any machine that can derive support in the atmosphere from the reactions of the air other than the reactions of the air against the earth's surface',[367] much of air law was made applicable to vehicles qualifying as aircraft.[368] Likewise, the application of criminal air law such as per the 1963 Tokyo Convention[369] or private air law as per the 1999 Montreal Convention[370] is fundamentally triggered by the involvement of an aircraft on board of which the criminal acts are conducted respectively the damage has occurred.

This should already warn against straightforward applicability of air law to manned spaceflight. The sovereignty over airspace, the foundation of all air law, is absent in outer space as a consequence of Article II of the Outer Space Treaty, which means that the foundation of space law is the conceptual opposite, namely the principled freedom of exploration and use of the area concerned.[371] In contrast to the notion of 'aircraft', 'space object', the other triggering concept of much of space law, has not really been defined by treaty law,[372] but has come to be generally seen as referring to 'any man-made object which is at least

---

1953 No. 8; Cmd. 6614; ATS 1957 No. 5; ICAO Doc. 7500; and the International Air Transport Agreement, Chicago, done 7 December 1944, entered into force 8 February 1945; 171 UNTS 387; 59 Stat. 1701; ICAO Doc. App. IV-2187.

367 *E.g.* Annex 7 to the Chicago Convention (*supra* n. 125), Aircraft Nationality and Registration Marks, 5th edition, July 2003, Definitions; Annex 8, Airworthiness of Aircraft, 10th edition, April 2005, Definitions.

368 *Cf. e.g.* Arts. 5, 7, 11, 12, 31, 32 & 37, Chicago Convention (*supra* n. 125).

369 Convention on Offences and Certain Other Acts Committed on Board Aircraft (hereafter Tokyo Convention), Tokyo, done 14 September 1963, entered into force 4 December 1969; 704 UNTS 219; TIAS 6768; UKTS 1969 No. 126; Cmnd. 2261; ATS 1970 No. 14; 2 ILM 1042 (1963); ICAO Doc. 8364.

370 Convention for the Unification of Certain Rules for International Carriage by Air (hereafter Montreal Convention), Montreal, done 28 May 1999, entered into force 4 November 2003; 2242 UNTS 350; ICAO Doc. 9740; S. Treaty Doc. No. 106-45; 48 *Zeitschrift für Luft- und Weltraumrecht* 326 (1999).

371 This, of course, also raised the issue of where the boundary between the sovereignty-subject areas of airspace and the global commons of outer space would have to be drawn; while no worldwide consensus exists in this regard (or even regarding the need to have a clear boundary in the first place), increasing convergence of individual States' opinions on an altitude of 100 km may be discerned; see *e.g.* F.G. von der Dunk, *Citius, Altius, Fortius* – Regulating Commercial Spaceflight under Air Law or Space Law?', in *Harmonising Regulatory and Antitrust Regimes for International Air Transport* (Ed. J. Walulik) (2019), 114; *cf.* however also the very detailed analysis in T. Gangale, *How High the Sky?* (2019).

372 *Cf.* the semi-circular, half-baked 'definition' of 'space object' as per Art. I(d), Liability Convention (*supra* n. 15): 'The term "space object" includes component parts of a space object as well as its launch vehicle and parts thereof'.

attempted to be physically brought into outer space',[373] which triggers both (again) the question of where outer space 'begins' and the potential for overlap with the definition of 'aircraft', as the one definition does not necessarily exclude the other.

Nevertheless, following the capture by Scaled Composites of the 2004 X-Prize[374] (which proved the viability of private sub-orbital flight) and then the NASA-supported development of private space vehicles with orbital capabilities to serve the ISS,[375] the emergence of private commercial space transportation, including in particular manned spaceflight, started to become almost inevitable, and the discussion on the applicability and application of air law became a major part of the broader discussions on how to regulate this new sector.

There are essentially two aspects to this discussion. On the one hand, it is clear that commercial spaceflight will, in operational terms, inevitably interfere with 'classical' aviation: on their way to and back from outer space the vehicles used for those activities will cross airspaces used, sometimes very intensively, by aircraft, and in many cases commercial spaceflight vehicles will also make use of existing airports.[376]

As to the first, that problem arose of course, at least in principle, as soon as the Space Age began. However, given the relatively low frequencies of space launches and the overwhelming public character thereof, certainly initially, the resulting safety issues of crossing potential aircraft paths could be solved basically on an *ad hoc* basis – by clearing the launch area, including surrounding airspace, for the duration of the launch window. If, however, spaceflight is going to become a far more frequent, perhaps even regular operation, undertaken moreover by (other) commercial companies, the airline industry might justifiably

---

[373] Von der Dunk, *supra* n. 55, 87.
[374] See further Von der Dunk, *supra* n. 73, 663–4, 672–82; S. Chaddha, U.S. Commercial Space Sector: Matured and Successful, 36 *Journal of Space Law* (2010), 29–32; *Suborbital Reusable Launch Vehicles and Emerging Markets*, FAA, February 2005, 1, 4–5.
[375] See further Von der Dunk, *supra* n. 73, 664–5, 702–5; *The Annual Compendium of Commercial Space Transportation: 2012*, FAA, February 2013, 33–5, 140–2.
[376] See M. Köster, Legal Problems Related to a Combined Use of Airspace by Air- and Spacecraft, in *'Project 2001' – Legal Framework for the Commercial Use of Outer Space* (Ed. K.H. Böckstiegel) (2002), 103–8; also Chaddha, *supra* n. 374, 34–9; T. Brannen, Private Commercial Space Transportation's Dependence on Space Tourism and NASA's Responsibility to Both, 75 *Journal of Air Law and Commerce* (2010), 652–60.

balk at being regularly confronted with additional burdens to accommodate such commercial space operations.

As to the second, only now, with technologies developed for private commercial spaceflight which make use of horizontal take-off and landing capabilities and procedures, have airports come to be a potential part of such operations as well, calling for proper and safe integration thereof in standard airport operations.

On the other hand, the issue becomes more fundamentally complicated when it comes to regulating the spacecraft to be used for sub-orbital or even orbital flights themselves, as well as their operations and technologies.

Much of the technology in particular for the first phases of the flight profile comes straight out of aviation – or, for example in the case of Virgin Galactic, simply includes an aircraft as a 'first stage' vehicle. In a later phase, furthermore, some of the technologies are intended to be used for point-to-point aviation-like transportation across the globe. Here, the space part of the trajectory is more like a helpful incident than a main target of the flight.[377]

Yet, at the same time the aim of all such flights is to reach at least the lower parts of that area of outer space. And whilst even the plans currently close to realization already vary from air-launched second-stage spacecraft to single-stage horizontal take-off vehicles, all of them make use of some form of rocket propulsion for the middle section of the flight profile. Whether for fun, for astronaut training or for scientific experiments, all prospective operators present micro-gravity as a major selling point of their ventures. Some in addition also advertise selling points such as views of the curvature of the earth and the atmosphere. All of these are elements typically associated with spaceflight. Markets to be targeted concern the servicing of public (as has already happened with the ISS) or private (Bigelow's future space hotels[378]) destinations orbiting in outer space.

---

377 *Cf.* also S.R. Freeland, Fly Me to the Moon: How will International Law Cope with Commercial Space Tourism, 11 *Melbourne Journal of International Law* (2010), 91–3, 96–9.
378 *Cf. The Annual Compendium of Commercial Space Transportation: 2012*, FAA, February 2013, 36; further B. Perlman, Grounding U.S. Commercial Space Regulation in the Constitution, 100 *The Georgetown Law Journal* (2012), 938–9.

In short, there is no obvious answer as to whether the regime to be developed for private commercial spaceflight itself (as opposed to taking care of the interaction of such activities with 'normal' aviation) should essentially follow space law or air law. Here one may note furthermore that in the short term the realization of an *international* regime for such spaceflight activities is neither likely nor necessary, given that all relevant projects so far are being developed within the United States, by US operators benefitting from US government investments, and both departing from US territory and landing there, whilst in between either remaining (as for sub-orbital flights) above US territory and airspace or traveling (as for orbital flights) to and from US space objects or the unique, US-led ISS built around US modules. This also means that it is quite likely that any such international regime would develop based on, or as a reaction to the approach of the United States as the one country that, because of these developments, was forced to address the issue in some detail by way of domestic law and regulation.

Some efforts to take the 'air law-approach' in preparation for commercial spaceflight were nevertheless undertaken at the international level as well. Notably, already in the early 2000s the International Civil Aviation Organization (ICAO) started to investigate whether sub-orbital flights would not have to be addressed under the Chicago Convention and/or ICAO authority.[379] In 2005 a report resulted[380] which, while pointing out that at least some of the sub-orbital vehicles on the drawing board fit within the definition of 'aircraft', desisted from urging the development of any further Standards and Recommended Practices (SARPs), which would have been the logical consequence of application of that definition.[381]

Still, given that some of the early initiators of manned spaceflight projects came from Europe, such an approach of addressing private commercial spaceflight from the vantage point of aviation rather than spaceflight was initially further developed by the European Aviation Safety Agency (EASA),[382] which investigated in greater

---

379 See P. van Fenema, Suborbital Flights and ICAO, 30 *Air and Space Law* (2005), 396–405.
380 Working Paper on Concept of Suborbital Flights, ICAO Council, 175th Session, 30 May 2005, C-WP/12436.
381 See T.R. Hughes & E. Rosenberg, Space Travel Law (and Politics): The Evolution of the Commercial Space Launch Amendments Act of 2004, 31 *Journal of Space Law* (2005), 76–7; V.J. Vissepó, Legal Aspects of Reusable Launch Vehicles, 31 *Journal of Space Law* (2005), 179–85.
382 EASA was established by Regulation of the European Parliament and of the Council on common

detail in particular the possibility of applying a special version of the international aircraft certification regime to such sub-orbital flights. As of around 2010, however, these efforts seem to have been silently shelved.[383]

Conversely, the United States has essentially taken a space law approach to the issue, and chosen to regulate all such flights – including sub-orbital ones – by adapting the existing law regulating private commercial space launches to include private commercial flights (read launches into and re-entries from outer space) carrying humans on board. Only the future will tell whether this approach will be by and large copied by other countries interested in or forced to address the issue, ultimately resulting in the development of customary international law based on such State practice-*cum-opinio iuris*, or whether internationally speaking a fragmented legal environment will come into existence with different States choosing different options domestically.

In any event, back when the US government decided to stimulate private involvement in the launch service sector in general, earlier on, in 1984, it had adopted the Commercial Space Launch Act.[384] Most importantly, any private company with US nationality or launching from US territory was required to obtain a licence for each intended individual launch of an object into outer space from the licensing agency, the Office of the Associate Administrator for Commercial Space Transportation (usually referred to as the Office for Commercial Space Transportation, or 'OCST') within the Federal Aviation Authority.[385]

Once the advent of private manned spaceflight then became a distinct possibility, it was this regime that was adapted for the purpose. First, in 1998 the Commercial Space Act[386] was 'amended (...) to address liability and government indemnification concerns and to address

---

rules in the field of civil aviation and establishing a European Aviation Safety Agency, No. 1592/2002/EC, of 15 July 2002; OJ L 240/1 (2002).
383 For instance, the next paper by J.B. Marciacq *et al.*, charged with this investigation, Towards Regulating Suborbital Flights: An Updated EASA Approach, Paper IAC-10-D2.9.5, presented at the 61st International Astronautical Congress, Prague, 2010, turned out *not* to be published in the *Proceedings of the International Institute of Space Law 2010* (2011).
384 Commercial Space Launch Act, 30 October 1984, Public Law 98-575, 98th Congress, H.R. 3942; 98 Stat. 3055; *Space Law – Basic Legal Documents*, E.III.3.
385 See Sec. 50904(a), 51 U.S.C.
386 Commercial Space Act, 27 January 1998, Public Law 105-303, 105th Congress, H.R. 1702; 51 U.S.C. 50101; 112 Stat. 2843 (1998).

licensing authority for RLVs [reusable launch vehicles]',[387] thus allowing the OCST to start licensing re-entry operations in addition to launches. Second, the 2004 Commercial Space Launch Amendments Act[388] now applied the licensing obligation also to re-entry, allowing for full-fledged licensing of manned sub-orbital flights. Third, the 2015 Commercial Space Launch Competitiveness Act[389] amended the relevant Section 50914(b)(1) of the Commercial Space Launch Act by including 'spaceflight participants' (effectively the passengers) in the existing cross-waiver of liability, meaning that there is no statutory obligation to accept contractual liability on the part of the spaceflight operators *vis-à-vis* such spaceflight participants.[390]

If private manned spaceflight operations had come to be regulated by US air law, following also from international obligations pursuant to the Chicago Convention and its Annexes, all this would have taken a different turn. First, it would not have been the OCST which would be in charge of the licensing process, but those parts of the FAA habitually certifying and licensing aircraft, airlines and crew. Second, this system would have included such detailed requirements as certification of airworthiness[391] and pilot licences,[392] rather than just a fairly general and broad licence to launch. Third, it would also have required the spaceflight operators to accept contractual liability *vis-à-vis* their passengers, which in aviation has been mandatory and subject to international harmonization ever since 1929.[393]

However, this development of commercial manned spaceflight regulation along the lines of space law currently remains confined to a single country, the United States, which has moreover included several

---

387 Hughes & Rosenberg, *supra* n. 381, 4.
388 Commercial Space Launch Amendments Act, 23 December 2004, Public Law 108-492, 108th Congress, H.R. 3752, 49 U.S.C.; 118 Stat. 3974.
389 *Supra* n. 216.
390 See further in great detail M.V. Carminati, *What Does Risk Mean in This New 'Risky Space Business'?* (2019).
391 Further to Arts. 29(b), 31, Chicago Convention (*supra* n. 125), as elaborated in Annex 8 on Airworthiness of Aircraft.
392 Further to Arts. 29(c), 32, Chicago Convention (*supra* n. 125), as elaborated in Annex 1 on Personnel Licensing.
393 This concerned the so-called Warsaw system originating with the 1929 Warsaw Convention (Convention for the Unification of Certain Rules Relating to International Transportation by Air, Warsaw, done 12 October 1929, entered into force 13 February 1933; 137 LNTS 11; USTS 876; UKTS 1933 No. 11; ATS 1963 No. 18); meanwhile, essentially this has been replaced by the 1999 Montreal Convention (*supra* n. 370).

relevant sunset clauses allowing the legislators to adapt a legal regime more akin to that of aviation once private commercial spaceflight matures, in particular from the current sub-orbital hops (amounting to little more than a sophisticated form of bungee jumping) to actual sub-orbital point-to-point transportation between major world population centres. This would also involve the need to address international aspects, such as traversing the upper parts of airspaces of other sovereign States, requiring their consent.

Also in other areas it may be helpful to use experience with aviation to draft further rules for commercial spaceflight, in the absence of useful rules or principles within the current *corpus iuris spatialis internationalis* to build upon.

For instance, once private commercial spaceflight became a more regular business, it would make sense to fundamentally integrate such flights into the prevalent system for air navigation, air space management and air traffic management services. Currently it seems too early for that, if only because it is as yet uncertain which of the various technologies being developed and tested in this context will ultimately make it to commercial maturity. For example, the level of manoeuvrability of a classical rocket launched vertically is considerably different from that of a spaceplane taking off horizontally, which should obviously direct relevant regulation trying to enhance safety.

In the same vein, once commercial space traffic becomes a more regular, perhaps even routine, feature, a version of traffic management for the higher echelons of airspace (so far usually not covered by concepts such as 'controlled (national) airspace') and the lower areas of outer space would also become necessary.[394] It would be rather unwise not to build such a system at least partially upon existing air traffic management regimes, while being careful to include the specifics of operating in outer space and/or in the context of space law properly into the equation.

Likewise, at such a level of maturity not only could certification and other standard-oriented safety legislation be introduced – such as already ultimately foreseen by the current US legal regime, provision-

---

394 See also F.G. von der Dunk, Space Traffic Management: A Challenge of Cosmic Proportions, in *Proceedings of the International Institute of Space Law 2015* (IISL) (2016), 385–96.

ally beyond 2023/2025[395] – but other elements of air law could be extended to relevant space vehicles as well, or used as guidance for the development of specific space law documents on the issue.

Another area where reference to air law regimes as a precedent or even possibly by extension an applicable set of rules might make sense concerning the criminal law aspects. Currently, the application of criminal air law (still) rests upon a combination of the applicability of the concepts of 'aircraft' respectively 'airspace'. The first treaty to address the issue was the aforementioned Tokyo Convention, which provided that the State in whose airspace an aircraft registered with another State is flying is the primary State entitled to exercise its 'criminal jurisdiction over an offence committed on board' – although the former State should not do so unless other criteria apply, namely if:

(a) the offence has effect on the territory of such State [being overflown];
(b) the offence has been committed by or against a national or permanent resident of such State;
(c) the offence is against the security of such State;
(d) the offence consists of a breach of any rules or regulations relating to the flight or maneuver of aircraft in force in such State; [or]
(e) the exercise of jurisdiction is necessary to ensure the observance of any obligation of such State under a multilateral international agreement.[396]

Additional treaties and protocols, such as the 1970 Hague Convention,[397] generally follow the same approach.

In other words, once and to the extent that the vehicles intended for use by private human spaceflight are considered 'aircraft', provided of course the various other requirements for application of the respective conventions were equally fulfilled, their respective regimes would also apply on board those private human spaceflight vehicles. It would require, nevertheless, an extension of scope, since not all vehicles to be used for private commercial spaceflight would currently qualify or even come close to qualifying as aircraft.

---

395 See Sec. 50905(c)(9), resp. Sec. 50915(f), 51 U.S.C.
396 Art. 4, in conjunction with Art. 1(2), Tokyo Convention (*supra* n. 369). See *e.g.* R. Abeyratne, ICAO's Involvement in Outer Space Affairs – A Need for Closer Scrutiny, 30 *Journal of Space Law* (2004), 190–3; Chatzipanagiotis, *supra* n. 88, 43–4.
397 Convention for the Suppression of Unlawful Seizure of Aircraft, The Hague, done 16 December 1970, entered into force 14 October 1971; 860 UNTS 105; TIAS 7192: ICAO Doc. 8920. *Cf.* further *e.g.* Abeyratne, *supra* n. 396, 190–3; Chatzipanagiotis, *supra* n. 88, 44–5.

Conversely, wherever future commercial spaceflight regimes would be developed on the basis of (existing) international space law, not only would basic clauses such as the absence of sovereignty as per Article II of the Outer Space Treaty, the general State responsibility and (perhaps) liability for private activities as per Articles VI and VII thereof and the Liability Convention continue to apply; other, more complex consequences would also have to be addressed. For instance, how would or should the Registration Convention be applied to such flights?[398] Or, to what extent would the Rescue Agreement apply to humans and objects involved in such spaceflights?[399]

Whatever ultimate, likely hybrid, regime will be developed on commercial manned spaceflight, it should essentially still continue to comply with the fundamentals of space law, in particular the structural core concepts of the *corpus iuris spatialis internationalis* as discussed above.[400]

5.4 The international trade regime for satellite communication services

The space treaties did not encompass any specific international trade-related clauses already, for the simple reason that in the 1960s and early 1970s the possibility of international commercial markets for space services was too remote to be taken on board during the drafting. Not even the term 'private' made it into the Outer Space Treaty; the concept was subsumed under the phrase 'non-governmental' used in Article VI.

Even as it became clear that satellite communications, the first and foremost application of space, was evolving into a multi-billion-dollar environment, it remained for a considerable time an arena for major international satellite organizations such as INTELSAT and INMARSAT[401] rather than for private operators. This paradigm only began to change in the mid-1980s, as in Europe (SES/Astra) and the

---

398 *Cf. e.g.* F.G. von der Dunk, Beyond *What?* Beyond *Earth Orbit?* ...! The Applicability of the Registration Convention to Private Commercial Manned *Sub-Orbital* Spaceflight, 43 *California Western International Law Journal* (2013), 269–341.
399 *Cf. e.g.* Sundahl, *supra* n. 88, 168–71, 177–89; Chatzipanagiotis, *supra* n. 88, 32, on the discussion about potential applicability of the Rescue Agreement (*supra* n. 30) to space tourists.
400 See *supra*, §§ 1.2, 1.3.
401 *Cf.* also *supra*, § 3.3.

United States (PanAmSat and OrionSat) the first major private operators entered the markets – and started complaining about having to compete on unfair terms with these intergovernmental behemoths.

In those two main telecommunications regions of the world, as well as other developed countries,[402] concurrently the perception grew that telecommunications in general, then also satellite communications in particular, should be provided not by the public sector but by the private industry and on a commercial basis. Consequently, it would also make sense to bring the international trade in such services within the scope of the international trade regime which had evolved from the 1947 General Agreement on Tariffs and Trade[403] to the 1994 establishment of the WTO[404] and the GATS,[405] the latter effectively transplanting the essence of the former to the area of trade in services (which was what telecommunications and satellite communications were mostly about) and adapting it as necessary in the process.

As for satellite communications, the 1994 GATS Annex on Telecommunications included this specific sector and thereby provided for the point of departure for liberalizing the international telecommunications markets, although as of yet excluding basic telecommunications.[406] Actual liberalization, however, depended on the application of the key principles of Most-Favoured-Nation (MFN)[407] respectively National Treatment (NT)[408] to the whole sector.

---

402 See further on this *supra*, § 3.3, esp. at n. 179.
403 Geneva, done 30 October 1947, entered into force 1 January 1948; 55 UNTS 194; TIAS 1700; ATS 1948 No. 23.
404 As per the WTO Agreement (*supra* n. 39). See further P.T. Stoll, World Trade Organization (WTO), in *The Max Planck Encyclopedia of Public International Law* (Ed. R. Wolfrum) *Vol. X* (2012), 968–90.
405 General Agreement on Trade in Services (hereafter GATS), Marrakesh, done 15 April 1994, entered into force 1 January 1995; 1869 UNTS 183; UKTS 1996 No. 58; Cm. 3276; ATS 1995 No. 8.
406 See Art. II(1), GATS (*supra* n. 405), Annex on Telecommunications & Annex on Negotiations on Basic Telecommunications. Further *e.g.* Bohlmann, Schrogl & Zilioli (*supra* n. 179), 220–27.
407 MFN prohibits the discrimination between services and service suppliers from different foreign States, unless exceptions apply, as 'each Member shall accord immediately and unconditionally to services and service suppliers of any other Member treatment no less favourable than that it accords to like services and service suppliers of any other country'; Art. II(1), GATS (*supra* n. 405).
408 NT prohibits the discrimination between services and service suppliers for foreign States and domestic services and service suppliers after having entered a specific national market, as 'each Member shall accord to services and service suppliers of any other Member, in respect of all measures affecting the supply of services, treatment no less favourable than that it accords to its own like services and service suppliers'; Art. XVII(1), GATS (*supra* n. 405).

The application of MFN to telecommunications was automatically achieved by the 1997 Fourth Protocol to the GATS,[409] which provided that

> a Schedule of Specific Commitments and a List of Exemptions from Article II concerning basic telecommunications annexed to this Protocol relating to a Member shall, in accordance with the terms specified therein, supplement or modify the Schedule of Specific Commitments and the List of Article II Exemptions of that Member.[410]

The application of NT conversely was still dependent on the individual Schedules of Specific Commitments mentioned above which were to be provided by the individual States. All such principles naturally applied on the basis of reciprocity: if one country imposed certain limits or conditions to the provision of services offered by a provider from another country, that other country could *vice versa* impose the same limits and conditions, even if not as such appearing in its own Schedule of Specific Commitments and hence not imposed on providers from third countries.

For the purpose of efficiency and coherence, telecommunication services were classified in 15 categories to be addressed by those Schedules of Specific Commitments which unequivocally included several categories of satellite communication services.

By way of the Fourth Protocol to the GATS and their attendant Schedules of Specific Commitments (together referred to as 'Agreement on Basic Telecommunications' or 'Agreement on Basic Telecommunication Services') then, at the time 54 WTO member States plus the European Commission on behalf of the then-15 EU member States, liberalized the global telecommunications market to the extent of covering more than 90% of global telecommunications revenues.

In terms of satellite communications, the Schedules of Specific Commitments provided for the substance of the liberalization achieved.

---

409 Fourth Protocol to the General Agreement on Trade and Services of 15 April 1994 (hereafter Fourth Protocol to the GATS), Geneva, done 15 April 1997, entered into force 5 February 1998; WTO Doc. S/L/20 of 30 April 1996 (96-1750); 2061 UNTS 209; ATS 1998 No. 9; 33 ILM 1167 (1994); 36 ILM 354 (1997).
410 Art. 1, Fourth Protocol to the GATS (*supra* n. 409).

In sum, 51 States (by way of 37 Schedules) committed themselves to allow foreign operators to offer some or all types of mobile satellite services or the related transport capacity in their national markets, while 50 States (by way of 36 Schedules) did so with respect to fixed satellite services or the transport capacity involved therein.

By now, the number of WTO member States having made such commitments in their schedules to allow international trade in telecommunication services within their territories has risen to 108.[411] In addition, 82 WTO member States have now committed to the regulatory principles of the WTO Reference Paper of 24 April 1996,[412] the policy paper which provided a major impetus to the establishment of the Fourth Protocol and the attendant schedules of commitments.

In sum, over the past decades within the framework established by the GATS a largely liberalized international trade environment for satellite services has evolved, including the largest developed economies of the world (the United States, the European Union, Japan, South Korea, Canada and Australia) as well as also including leading developing nations (China, Russia, India, Indonesia, South Africa, Nigeria, Mexico, Brazil and Argentina).

At the same time, it was a somewhat haphazard process leaving many individual idiosyncratic elements intact. This is mainly due to the system of Schedules of Specific Commitments and the complexity of service provision, which generally can take four forms, each subject to different parameters and issues, defined by the GATS as:

(a) from the territory of one Member into the territory of any other Member;
(b) in the territory of one Member to the service consumer of any other Member;
(c) by a service supplier of one Member, through commercial presence in the territory of any other Member; [or]
(d) by a service supplier of one Member, through presence of natural persons of a Member in the territory of any other Member.[413]

---

411 See https://www.wto.org/english/tratop_e/serv_e/telecom_e/telecom_e.htm (last accessed 16 June 2020).
412 Telecommunications Services; Reference Paper, Negotiating group on basic telecommunications, 24 April 1996; http://www.wto.org/english/tratop_e/serv_e/telecom_e/tel23_e.htm (last accessed 16 June 2020); see also https://www.wto.org/english/tratop_e/serv_e/telecom_e/telecom_e.htm (last accessed 16 June 2020).
413 Art. I(2), GATS (*supra* n. 405). Usually, those four categories are referred to as cross-border

Sometimes satellite communications are implicitly included in all or most of such commitments to liberalize foreign access to national markets, as per the MFN and NT principles; sometimes they are expressly singled out. In the latter case, moreover, they are often subject to specific but varying limitations concerning foreign equity in terms of commercial presence or obligatory use of national operators and/or facilities.[414] In many cases therefore only extended investigation and close inspection and analysis of the relevant commitment in the light of general GATS obligations allows for a final determination of the actual legal situation concerning the rights of foreign satellite service providers to a certain national market.

Whereas the WTO/GATS regime makes no specific reference to the UN treaties forming the core of space law, this is largely due to the fact that both regimes basically address fundamentally different aspects of the satellite communication activities subject to both: the space treaties focus on the in-space parts of the operations, dealing with registration of space objects, liability for damage and suchlike, whereas the WTO/GATS regime focuses on the post-space, downstream issues of market access for those satellite operations undertaken for commercial purposes. That, however, clearly does not mean that either the space treaties do not continue to apply also to satellite operations for commercial purposes, or the WTO/GATS regime would not be relevant for those satellite operations as part of space law *lato sensu*, since in the absence of feasible market opportunities relevant operators would be unlikely to undertake the relevant space activities in the first place.

5.5 Concluding remarks

While intellectual property rights, aviation and international trade relations and their respective international regimes may provide the most important examples of non-space legal regimes having a profound bearing on one or the other sector of space activities, there is

---

supply, consumption abroad, commercial presence and presence of natural persons respectively. See further A. Marsoof, A Case for *Sui Generis* Treatment of Software under the WTO Regime, 20 *International Journal of Law and Information Technology* (2012), 293–304; J. Bhagwati, Economic Perspective on Trade in Professional Services, in *Legal Problems of International Economic Relations* (Eds. J.H. Jackson, W.J. Davey & A.O. Sykes) (4th ed.) (2002), 855–8.

414 See for a more detailed overview *e.g.* Von der Dunk, *supra* n. 345, 848–52.

a whole range of other regimes which could be discussed under this heading as well.

Notably, somewhat similar to the involvement of air law in the context of private manned spaceflight, given the establishment of Sea Launch and its launch activities from the high seas, the law of the sea may have a considerable impact on the relevant space activities, concerning for instance the 'freedom to construct artificial islands and other installations permitted under international law' on the high seas, but not on the Continental Shelf – and its appropriate legal limitations, parameters and ramifications.[415]

On a different level, the legal order created by the European Union (EU),[416] going back to the late 1950s with the creation of the European Economic Community (EEC), until the mid-1980s did not in any distinguishable manner involve or address outer space or space activities.[417] However, it has since come to address in particular satellite communications,[418] and to some extent also for instance satellite remote sensing.[419] In particular following the 2007 Lisbon Treaty,[420] the Union now has some measure of competence in *all* realms of commercial space activities and applications.[421]

---

415 Art. 87(1)(d), United Nations Convention on the Law of the Sea (*supra* n. 9).
416 The European Union is currently based upon two key treaties: the Treaty on European Union as amended by the Treaty of Lisbon amending the Treaty on European Union and the Treaty establishing the European Community, Lisbon, done 13 December 2007, entered into force 1 December 2009; OJ C 326/13 (2012); and the Treaty establishing the European Community as amended by the Treaty of Lisbon amending the Treaty on European Union and the Treaty establishing the European Community, Lisbon, done 13 December 2007, entered into force 1 December 2009; OJ C 326/47 (2012).
417 See for origins and details of the European Union's involvement in outer space and space activities further Von der Dunk, *supra* n. 196, 239–67.
418 Pursuant to the 1994 Satellite Directive (*supra* n. 179), as already briefly touched upon *supra*, § 3.3.
419 Pursuant to the 1996 Database Directive (*supra* n. 354), as already briefly touched upon *supra*, § 5.2.
420 Treaty of Lisbon amending the Treaty on European Union and the Treaty establishing the European Community, Lisbon, done 13 December 2007, entered into force 1 December 2009; OJ C 306/1 (2007).
421 See on this further *e.g.* S. Hobe *et al.*, A New Chapter for Europe in Space, 54 *Zeitschrift für Luft- und Weltraumrecht* (2005), 336–56; F.G. von der Dunk, The EU Space Competence as per the Treaty of Lisbon: Sea Change or Empty Shell?, in *Proceedings of the International Institute of Space Law 2011* (2012), 382–92.

A final, yet fundamentally different example – and one mainly in the initial phases at that – concerns the application of international law regarding cultural artefacts and heritage sites to relevant items and venues on celestial bodies, such as remnants of the Apollo Moon landers and the areas around them, including the first footsteps of Neil Armstrong and Buzz Aldrin. While supposedly limited to terrestrial heritage sites, the Convention Concerning the Protection of the World Cultural and Natural Heritage[422] does not *ipso facto* exclude application to extra-terrestrial sites, although the main focus is on a State's duty to protect such sites 'situated on its territory',[423] noting again that of course there legally speaking *is* no territory in outer space.

Given the lack of specificity in all such treaties in the second ring, logically they would only apply within the parameters set by the core of the *corpus iuris spatialis internationalis*, as well as both parts of the first ring as more of a *lex specialis* compared with the *lex generalis* of this second ring – noting that, moreover, they would most likely require considerable adaptation to apply to outer space, space activities and space actors in a sensible manner.

---

[422] Convention Concerning the Protection of the World Cultural and Natural Heritage, Paris, done, 16 November 1972, entered into force 17 December 1975; 1037 UNTS 151.

[423] Art. 4, Convention Concerning the Protection of the World Cultural and Natural Heritage (*supra* n. 422).

6 The third ring: national space legislation

6.1 Introduction

National space legislation comprises all domestic laws, statutes, regulations and suchlike dealing with space, which *largo sensu* comprises legislation addressing exclusively and comprehensively space and space activities as the equivalent on the domestic level of the core of international space law but also the domestic equivalents of the first ring, both Northern and Southern parts, and second ring discussed before.

In such a sense, probably *all* States of the world would have some national legislation meeting this broad criterion, which obviously makes it impossible to treat them all here, even if we limited ourselves to a very high-level overview. Actually, even if we would exclude anything equivalent to the second ring or the Southern part of the first ring, the number of States concerned would be substantial – and continuously growing.

For instance, a number of countries have a national law specifically establishing a national space agency of some sort and/or endowing it with specific tasks, roles and competences. Major examples would concern the 1958 US National Aeronautics and Space Act establishing NASA,[424] the 1961 French Statute establishing CNES,[425] the 1991 Argentine Decree creating CONAE,[426] the 1992 Statute establishing

---

[424] National Aeronautics and Space Act, 29 July 1958, Public Law 85-568, 85th Congress, H.R. 12575; as amended through 1983; 72 Stat. 426; *Space Law – Basic Legal Documents*, E.III.1 (original instalment).

[425] *Statut du Centre National d'Etudes Spatiales*; Loi n° 61-1382 du 19 décembre 1961; *Journal Officiel de la République Française* (20 Déc. 1961), 11665; *National Space Legislation of the World*, Vol. I (2001), at 385.

[426] Creation of the National Commission on Space Activities, National Decree No. 995/91, 28 May 1991; *National Space Legislation of the World*, Vol. II (2002), at 366; *United Nations/Nigeria Workshop on Space Law, National Legislation and Policy – Selected Texts* (2005), at 6.

the Russian space agency[427] and the 1994 Law establishing the Brazilian space agency.[428]

Many other countries have national space legislation implementing specific elements or aspects of international space law. For example, some countries have dealt with the issue of space object registration domestically, ensuring exercise of jurisdiction and control over space objects. This currently concerns Germany,[429] Spain,[430] Argentina,[431] China[432] and Italy.[433] Italy also, to provide another example, has had legislation in force since 1983 addressing the relationship between Italy and its citizens in the case of claims under the Liability Convention where Italy could act as the claimant State.[434]

In the context of implementation of international space law however, the most important role of national space law, given the ever-growing involvement of private enterprise in the space sector, is to ensure that

---

427 Statute of the Russian Space Agency (RKA) (abbreviated version), approved by the Government of the Russian Federation, Decree of 9 April 1992; 20 *Journal of Space Law* 106 (1992).

428 Law Establishing the Brazilian Space Agency, No. 8.854, of 10 February 1994; http://www.planalto.gov.br/ccivil_03/leis/L8854.htm (last accessed 16 June 2020).

429 Actually, this is achieved as per the Civil Aviation Act (*Luftverkehrsgesetz*), originally adopted in 1922, as revised most recently 11 December 2008; Federal Law Gazette I, at 2418; German Civil Aviation Act (2009), at 17.

430 Royal Decree No. 278/1995 establishing in the Kingdom of Spain of the Registry foreseen in the Convention adopted by the United Nations General Assembly on 2nd November 1974, 24 February 1995, Prime Minister's Chancellery; *United Nations/Nigeria Workshop on Space Law, National Legislation and Policy – Selected Texts* (2005), at 201; http://www.unoosa.org/oosa/en/ourwork/spacelaw/nationalspacelaw/spain/royal_decree_278_1995E.html (last accessed 16 June 2020).

431 Establishment of the National Registry of Objects Launched into Outer Space, National Decree No. 125/95, 19 July 1995; *National Space Legislation of the World*, Vol. II (2002), at 373; *United Nations/Nigeria Workshop on Space Law, National Legislation and Policy – Selected Texts* (2005), at 10.

432 Order No. 6 of the Commission of Science, Technology, and Industry for National Defense and the Ministry of Foreign Affairs of the People's Republic of China, Measures for the Administration of Registration of Objects Launched into Outer Space, of 8 February 2001; unofficial English translation 33 *Journal of Space Law* (2007), 437.

433 Law on Accession of the Italian Republic to the Convention on the registration of objects launched in outer space, made in New York on 14 January 1975 and its execution (*Legge 'Adesione della Repubblica italiana alla Convenzione sull'immatricolazione sugli oggetti lanciati nello spazio extra-atmosferico, fatta a New York il 14 gennaio 1975 e sua esecuzione'*), Nr. 153, 12 July 2005; *Gazzetta Ufficiale* Nr. 177 of 1 August 2005.

434 Norms for the implementation for the Convention on International Liability for Damage caused by Space Objects, signed in London, Moscow and Washington 29 March 1972, Nr. 23, 25 January 1983; *Gazzetta Ufficiale* 35 of 5 February 1983; unofficial English translation https://download.esa.int/docs/ECSL/Italy2.pdf (last accessed 16 June 2020).

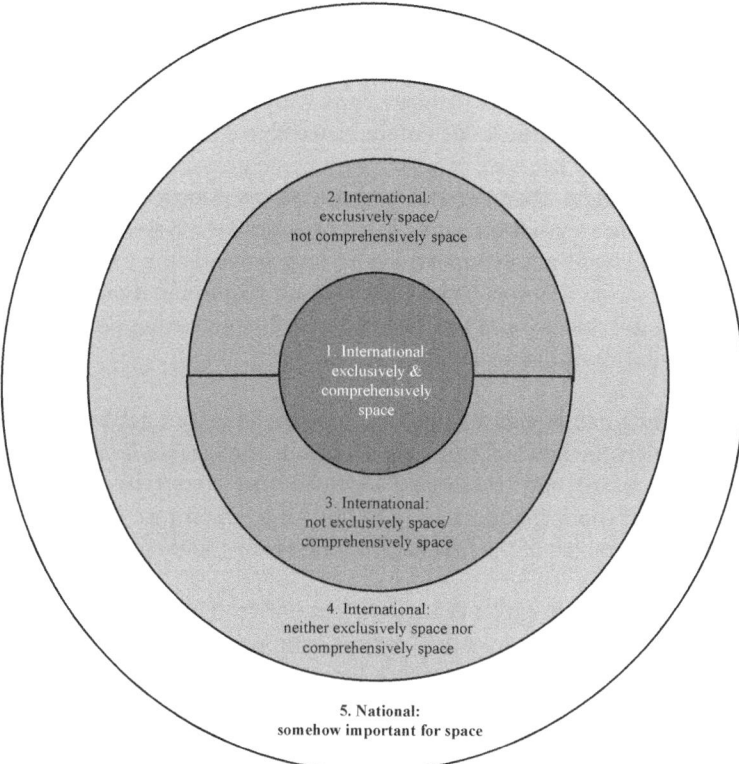

Figure 6.1 The third ring: national space legislation

its activities will also be undertaken in compliance with the substance of international space law.[435] This is, therefore, what the present chapter will briefly address (Figure 6.1).

6.2 National space legislation addressing private sector space activities

The role of national space legislation in addressing private sector space activities links back to the structural provisions of the Outer Space

---

[435] See in general on national space legislation also as for substantive elements Marboe, *supra* n. 77, 127–204; Von der Dunk, *supra* n. 7; *National Regulation of Space Activities* (Ed. R.S. Jakhu) (2010); *National Space Legislation in Europe* (Ed. F.G. von der Dunk) (2011); *Nationales Weltraumrecht/*

Treaty as discussed before,[436] with Article VI providing for State responsibility for private sector activities in outer space as well as requiring their authorization and continuing supervision, and Article VII providing for State liability for damage caused by private sector activities, attributed through the launch of the space object causing the damage.

From that angle, there would currently be 28 countries which have national space legislation in place that provides for a system of authorization and continuing supervision[437] of private sector entities, thus fulfilling most comprehensively the relevant requirement of Article VI of the Outer Space Treaty while also, by and large, taking care of State responsibility and State liability.

The most fundamental distinction to be made is that between countries which (in line with the inner core of the *corpus iuris spatialis internationalis*) have essentially addressed the comprehensive space sector, and those that have only by and large taken care (in line with the Northern part of the first ring) of one or the other space sector.

Somewhat in between is the special case of the United States, which has the by far most extended body of national space legislation, but, addressing specific sectors of interest to the private sector only once such interests have started materializing, has a disparate set of statutes and federal regulations resulting in a complex regulatory landscape.

This development essentially started in 1970, when the 1934 Communications Act,[438] providing for a licensing regime for private communication operators, was formally declared to apply to operators

---

National Space Law (Eds. C. Brünner & E. Walter) (2008); Reif, Schmidt-Tedd & Wannenmacher (*supra* n. 7), 411–28; M. Gerhard & K.U. Schrogl, Report of the 'Project 2001' Working Group on National Space Legislation, in *'Project 2001' – Legal Framework for the Commercial Use of Outer Space* (Ed. K.H. Böckstiegel) (2002), 532–58.

436 See *supra*, § 1.2.

437 The term 'authorization' should be understood in a general sense; many countries and their laws and regulations refer not to 'authorizations' but to 'licences', 'permissions', 'permits', 'approvals' and/or other similar terms, respectively their translation into the national language, but they would all boil down to the same: the consent of a relevant sovereign State given to private sector entities to conduct certain space activities subject to certain conditions. For the sake of this analysis, 'supervision' is conceived as merely a specific part or extension of the concept of 'authorization', since any national space law providing details on supervision of non-governmental entities' space activities almost by definition applies those to activities (to be) authorized by the same regime. See also *e.g.* Marboe, *supra* n. 77, 134–5.

438 Communications Act, 19 June 1934; 47 U.S.C. 151 (1988); 48 Stat. 1064.

using satellites as part of their operational infrastructure.[439] As of 1984, both private launch service providers[440] and private remote sensing satellite operators[441] could also obtain licences for their respective operations. While some efforts were made to establish a little more coherence in this fragmented landscape by way of the 1998 Commercial Space Act,[442] it was the 2015 Commercial Space Launch Competitiveness Act[443] that addressed in its Title IV the up-and-coming space resource mining industry, albeit in a very embryonic fashion.

Nineteen other countries (including one actually a region within another State) then *have* basically covered the whole space sector. In chronological order this concerns Sweden (as of 1982),[444] the UK (as of 1986),[445] South Africa (as of 1993),[446] the Russian Federation (also as of 1993),[447] Ukraine (as of 1996),[448] Belgium (as of 2005),[449] the Netherlands

---

439 Communications Satellite Facilities, *First Report and Order*, 22 FCC 2d 86 (1970), Appendix C, p. 1.
440 By way of the Commercial Space Launch Act (*supra* n. 384). It was this Act which was later extended to also apply to *manned* space launches, including those for purposes of space tourism; see further *supra*, § 5.3.
441 By way of the Land Remote-Sensing Commercialization Act, 17 July 1984, Public Law 98-365, 98th Congress, H.R. 5155; 98 Stat. 451; *Space Law – Basic Legal Documents*, E.III.4; later amended by the Land Remote Sensing Policy Act, 28 October 1992, Public Law 102-555, 102nd Congress, H.R. 6133; 15 U.S.C. 5601; 106 Stat. 4163.
442 *Supra*, n. 386.
443 *Supra*, n. 216.
444 Act on Space Activities, 1982: 963, 18 November 1982; *National Space Legislation of the World*, Vol. I (2001), at 398; *Space Law – Basic Legal Documents*, E.II.1; 36 *Zeitschrift für Luft- und Weltraumrecht* (1987), at 11; and Decree on Space Activities, 1982: 1069; *National Space Legislation of the World*, Vol. I (2001), at 399; *Space Law – Basic Legal Documents*, E.II.2; 36 *Zeitschrift für Luft- und Weltraumrecht* (1987), at 11.
445 Outer Space Act, 18 July 1986, 1986 Chapter 38; *National Space Legislation of the World*, Vol. I (2001), at 293; *Space Law – Basic Legal Documents*, E.I; 36 *Zeitschrift für Luft- und Weltraumrecht* (1987), 12; later complemented by the Space Industry Act, 15 March 2018, 2018 Chapter 5; http://www.legislation.gov.uk/ukpga/2018/5/contents/enacted (last accessed 16 June 2020).
446 Space Affairs Act, 6 September 1993, assented to on 23 June 1993, No. 84 of 1993; Statutes of the Republic of South Africa – Trade and Industry, Issue No. 27, 21–44; *National Space Legislation of the World*, Vol. I (2001), at 413.
447 Law of the Russian Federation on Space Activities, No. 5663-1, 20 August 1993, effective 6 October 1993; *National Space Legislation of the World*, Vol. I (2001), at 101; *United Nations/Nigeria Workshop on Space Law, National Legislation and Policy – Selected Texts* (2005), at 162.
448 Law of Ukraine on Space Activities, No. 502/96-VR, 15 November 1996; *National Space Legislation of the World*, Vol. I (2001), at 36; *United Nations/Nigeria Workshop on Space Law, National Legislation and Policy – Selected Texts* (2005), at 205.
449 Law on the Activities of Launching, Flight Operations or Guidance of Space Objects, of 17 September 2005; *Nationales Weltraumrecht/National Space Law* (2008), at 183; *United Nations/Nigeria Workshop on Space Law, National Legislation and Policy – Selected Texts* (2005), at 92.

(as of 2007),[450] France (as of 2008),[451] Nigeria (as of 2010),[452] Austria (as of 2011),[453] Kazakhstan (as of 2012),[454] Indonesia (as of 2013),[455] Denmark (as of 2016),[456] Japan (as of 2016),[457] Greece (as of 2017),[458] Finland (as of 2018),[459] Portugal (as of 2019)[460] and the United Arab Emirates (as of 2019).[461] Finally, there is the unique case of Hong Kong,[462] as of 1997 strictly speaking applying a *regional* space law as opposed to a *national* one, but still essentially regulating private space activities.

In addition, so far only five countries have national space legislation explicitly or implicitly focusing on the launch sector, for a large part

---

450 Law Incorporating Rules Concerning Space Activities and the Establishment of a Registry of Space Objects, 24 January 2007; 80 *Staatsblad* (2007), at 1; *Nationales Weltraumrecht/National Space Law* (2008), at 201.

451 Law on Space Operations (*Loi relative aux opérations spatiales*); *Loi n° 2008-518 du 3 juin 2008*; unofficial English translation 34 *Journal of Space Law* (2008), 453.

452 National Space Research and Development Agency Act, adopted 27 August 2010, No. 9 of 2010; Federal Republic of Nigeria Gazette No. 98 of 30 August 2010, A 1249–68.

453 Federal Law on the Authorisation of Space Activities and the Establishment of a National Space Registry (*Bundesgesetz über die Genehmigung von Weltraumaktivitäten und die Einrichtung eines Weltraumregisters (Weltraumgesetz)*), as adopted by Parliament on 6 December 2011; Federal Law Gazette of 27 December 2011; 61 *Zeitschrift für Luft- und Weltraumrecht* (2012), 37–42, 56–61.

454 Law of the Republic of Kazakhstan on Space Activities, of 6 January 2012, 2012 No. 528-IV; https://www.unoosa.org/documents/pdf/spacelaw/national/kazakhstan/528-IV_2012-01-06E.pdf (last accessed 16 June 2020).

455 Law of the Republic of Indonesia on Space Activities, Nr. 21, of 6 August 2013; State Gazette of the Republic of Indonesia (2013), Nr. 133.

456 Outer Space Act (*Lov om aktiviteter i det ydre rum*), passed by Parliament with the third treatment, 3 May 2016; Parliament Gazette, 2015-17, No. L 128.

457 Space Activities Act, Act No. 76 of 2016.

458 Law no. 4508; Licensing of space activities – Registration in the National Register of Space Objects – Establishment of Hellenic Space Agency and other provisions; Government Gazette of the Hellenic Republic, 22 December 2017, Issue no. A 200; https://www.hellenicparliament.gr/UserFiles/bcc26661-143b-4f2d-8916-0e0e66ba4c50/a-diasth-pap-aposp.pdf (in Greek only; last accessed 16 June 2020).

459 Act on Space Activities, 63/2018, of 23 January 2018; http://tem.fi/documents/1410877/3227301/Act+on+Space+Activities/a3f9c6c9-18fd-4504-8ea9-bff1986fff28/Act+on+Space+Activities.pdf (last accessed 16 June 2020).

460 Decree-Law No. 16/2019, of 22 January 2019; Official Journal, 1st Series – No. 15, of 22 January 2019; https://www.vda.pt/xms/files/05_Publicacoes/2019/Flashes_Newsletters/Portuguese_Space_Act.pdf (last accessed 16 June 2020).

461 See *supra*, n. 216.

462 Outer Space Ordinance, An Ordinance to confer licensing and other powers on the Chief Executive to secure compliance with the international obligations of the People's Republic of China with respect to the launching and operation of space objects and the carrying on of other activities in outer space, 13 June 1997, as amended 1999, Chapter 523; *National Space Legislation of the World*, Vol. II (2002), at 403; 51 *Zeitschrift für Luft- und Weltraumrecht* (2002), 50.

owing to the focus of the international liability regime on space objects launched causing damage:[463] Norway (as of 1969),[464] Australia (as of 1998),[465] Brazil (as of 2001),[466] South Korea (as of 2005)[467] and New Zealand (as of 2017).[468] Two countries established such a regime addressing private sector participation in remote sensing only, mainly to address potential national security issues involved – Canada (as of 2005)[469] and Germany (as of 2007)[470] – whereas one country so far only has a national space law dealing with prospective interests by private parties in space resource exploitation – Luxembourg (as of 2017).[471]

6.3 Scope and approach of national space legislation

The important role of national space legislation in applying and implementing international space law, and by that token also in certain cases

---

463 See further *supra*, § 2.4.
464 Act on launching objects from Norwegian territory into outer space, No. 38, 13 June 1969; *National Space Legislation of the World*, Vol. I (2001), at 286; *United Nations/Nigeria Workshop on Space Law, National Legislation and Policy – Selected Texts* (2005), at 159.
465 An act about space activities, and for related purposes, No. 123 of 1998, assented to 21 December 1998; *National Space Legislation of the World*, Vol. I (2001), at 197. This Act has been repeatedly amended substantially since.
466 Administrative Edict No. 27, 20 June 2001; *National Space Legislation of the World*, Vol. II (2002), at 377; including the Regulation on procedures and on definition of necessary requirements for the request, evaluation, issuance, follow-up and supervision of licences for carrying out launching space activities on Brazilian territory.
467 Space Development Promotion Act, Law No. 7538, of 31 May 2005, entered into force 1 December 2005; unofficial English translation 33 *Journal of Space Law* (2007), 175; https://www.unoosa.org/oosa/en/ourwork/spacelaw/nationalspacelaw/republic_of_korea/space_development_promotions_actE.html (last accessed 16 June 2020); soon followed by the Space Liability Act, Law No. 8852, of 21 December 2007; UNOOSA National Space Law Database, https://www.unoosa.org/documents/pdf/spacelaw/national/Korean-Space-Liability-Act-unauthorized-translated-version.pdf (last accessed 16 June 2020).
468 Outer Space and High-altitude Activities Act 2017, No. 29 of 2017, assented to 10 July 2017, entered into force 21 December 2017; http://www.legislation.govt.nz/act/public/2017/0029/48.0/whole.html#DLM7312701 (last accessed 16 June 2020).
469 Remote Sensing Space Systems Act, assented to 25 November 2005; S.C. 2005, c. 45; soon followed by the Remote Sensing Space Systems Regulations, 29 March 2007; SOR/2007-66.
470 Act Protecting Against the Endangerment of German Security Through the Proliferation of High Resolution Aerial Imagery of the Earth (*Satellitendatensicherheitsgesetz*), 23 November 2007, effective 1 December 2007; Federal Gazette (*BGBl.*) Year 2007 Part I No. 58, of 28 November 2007.
471 See *supra*, n. 216. Note however that at the time of writing Luxembourg is also in the process of adopting a national space law covering in principle *all* private space activities.

helping to interpret the latter, was most prominently recognized by the National Space Legislation Resolution.[472]

The Resolution, first, called for comprehensive application *ratione materiae* of any such national space law, given *inter alia* the comprehensive scope of the notion 'activities in outer space' of Article VI of the Outer Space Treaty, as such law should

> include, as appropriate, the launch of objects into and their return from outer space, the operation of a launch or re-entry site and the operation and control of space objects in orbit; other issues for consideration may include the design and manufacture of spacecraft, the application of space science and technology, and exploration activities and research.[473]

Including for the moment the United States, 20 out of the 28 countries referenced above have indeed more or less complied with this strong recommendation, whereby in the case of some of the others it might be assumed that private space activities other than those regulated would meet with major obstacles – if indeed allowed. Also, more generally those 28 include most of the important spacefaring nations.[474]

Still, it leaves an overwhelming numerical majority of countries worldwide, including major spacefaring nations such as China, India, Mexico, Argentina, Italy and Spain, without any such national space legislation, even while (with the possible exception of China) principally qualifying as free market economies.

In terms of implementing the obligation following from Article VI of the Outer Space Treaty and the strong push resulting from Article VII of the Outer Space Treaty in conjunction with the Liability Convention, therefore, a lot of work still needs to be done. Part of the reason for this absence of national space legislation in so many countries may be the lack of clarity of the concept of '*national* activities in outer space' for which States may be held responsible under Article VI,[475] and of that of

---

472 *Supra* n. 54; see further I. Marboe, S. Aoki & T. Brisibe, The 2013 Resolution on Recommendations on National Space Legislation Relevant to the Peaceful Exploration and Use of Outer Space, in *Cologne Commentary on Space Law* (Eds. S. Hobe, B. Schmidt-Tedd & K.U. Schrogl) *Vol. III* (2015), 483–603.
473 No. 1, National Space Legislation Resolution (*supra* n. 54).
474 In addition, it may be noted that a handful of other States is currently developing a national space law.
475 Some authors have argued that it effectively meant 'activities of nationals' (only), following the use

the 'launching State' which may make States liable under Article VII and the Liability Convention,[476] leaving them to assume they would *not* be held responsible and/or liable where they might well turn out to be held so responsible or liable.

As for the former, luckily the National Space Legislation Resolution has now essentially solved the issue of the scope *materiae personae* of the responsibility under Article VI, in that it provides:

> The State, taking into account its obligations as a launching State and as a State responsible for national activities in outer space under the United Nations treaties on outer space, should ascertain national jurisdiction over space activities *carried out from territory under its jurisdiction and/or control*; likewise, it should issue authorizations for and ensure supervision over space activities *carried out elsewhere by its citizens and/or legal persons established, registered or seated in territory under its jurisdiction and/or control*, provided, however, that if another State is exercising jurisdiction with respect to such activities, the State should consider forbearing from duplicative requirements and avoid unnecessary burdens.[477]

An analysis of the 28 States already briefly discussed reveals that, indeed, the overwhelming majority now applies, in conformity with the Resolution's strong suggestion, both territorial and national jurisdiction for their domestic systems of authorization and continuing supervision, the few exceptions presenting rather idiosyncratic approaches.[478]

As for the latter, unfortunately no such solution is offered. Neither the National Space Legislation Resolution, nor the Launching State

---

of the concept of 'nationals' in Art. IX, Outer Space Treaty (*supra* n. 4); others that it essentially should equate with cases where a State also qualifies as a State liable for damage in accordance with Art. VII, Outer Space Treaty, and Art. I(c)(ii), Liability Convention (*supra* n. 15) whereas a third group essentially equated national activities for which a State can be held responsible with those over which it is entitled to exercise some form of generally accepted jurisdiction – meaning, at least, the activities of those entities with the nationality of that State and of those operating from the territory (and quasi-territory) of that State; see further Von der Dunk, *supra* n. 55, 53–4.

476 It is for instance unclear to what extent a *private* entity launching a space object, procuring the launch thereof or allowing its facility to be used for the launch thereof makes a State liable under that particular heading; see further Von der Dunk, *supra* n. 55, 83–4.

477 No. 2, National Space Legislation Resolution (*supra* n. 54); emphasis added.

478 See further F.G. von der Dunk, Scoping National Space Law: The True Meaning of 'National Activities in Outer Space' of Article VI of the Outer Space Treaty, to be published in *Proceedings of the International Institute of Space Law 2019*, in 2020.

Resolution (in spite of recommending 'that States (...) in fulfilling their international obligations under the United Nations treaties on outer space (...) consider enacting and implementing national laws authorizing and providing for continuing supervision of the activities in outer space of non-governmental entities under their jurisdiction'[479]) provide any further detail as to the proper scope *ratione personae* of the liability under Article VII and the Liability Convention.

Consequently, some States apply their regime of authorization and supervision to launches procured by private entities as if they procured those launches themselves, while others do not; some require authorization from their nationals for the operation of launch facilities regardless of where they operate them, others do not.[480]

Not surprisingly, on other more substantive respects the national space laws and regulations adopted so far provide an even more disparate spectrum, for instance when it comes to the extent to which the liability, unlimited at the international level, is also to be reimbursed by an authorized operator without limit and, if not, what the limit is or how that limit is to be calculated – and then, to what extent insurance against such derogated liability is required.[481]

6.4 Concluding remarks

While the considerable diversity of national space legislation, even when taking into account only the 28 countries which have so far some version of a comprehensive authorization system in place, is to be expected, given the lack of precision of the core of international space law and the sovereignty of individual States still being the main legal concept in international space law, the question then arises whether this diversity presents a problem.

The risk of a resulting 'race to the bottom', of 'flags of convenience' arising with detrimental effect on the accessibility of outer space and the benefits of space activities for humankind may not be as large as it might probably seem at first glance, mainly for two reasons: (1) space

---

479 No. 1, Launching State Resolution (*supra* n. 52).
480 See further *e.g.* Marboe, *supra* n. 77, 137–78.
481 See *e.g.* F.G. von der Dunk, Towards 'Flags of Convenience' in Space?, in *Proceedings of the International Institute of Space Law 2012* (2013), 818–22.

objects launched from the territory of one State would be likely first and most of all to harm *that* State, and (2) the beauty of the Liability Convention, stemming from the comprehensive system of State liability for privately caused damage, very much makes it a legal problem for the launching State(s) rather than the victims if private operators are not made subject to licensing requirements with a certain rigorousness to them.[482] Both may conspire to provide a serious check on any temptation to become a 'flag of convenience'.

The risks of such developments may, therefore, lie more in a fragmentation of the international 'market' for commercial space services, with individual operators, their clients and other stakeholders seeing themselves confronted with a bewildering array of possible or actual scenarios which may, in first instance, come to pose economic burdens, and then perhaps, indirectly, also give rise to more safety- and security-related risks.

While the likelihood of international space law being able to substantially address any such problems does not look particularly substantial – noting also that any possibility for international trade law to be used for such a purpose in the current geopolitical landscape is rather remote – it may be the only way nevertheless, if the general aims and goals of the space treaties are to be upheld, and (the exploration and use of) outer space is indeed to remain the 'province of all mankind'.[483]

---

482 See further Von der Dunk, *supra* n. 481, 826–8.
483 Art. I, Outer Space Treaty (*supra* n. 4).

7 The future of space law

As an old Danish proverb apparently had it: 'It is difficult to make predictions, especially about the future'.[484] That obviously applies also to space law, given the rapidity of developments in the space arena. It is barely 60 years ago that the Soviet Union sent a tiny metal sphere into outer space being able to do little more than go 'beep-beep-beep' – and today we are already completely used to sending Internet messages across the globe, forecasting the weather and navigating anything from bombs to aircraft to hikers, usually not even realizing anymore that it is space technology that helps us to do that. And if certain visionaries are to be believed, within the next few decades we will see space tourism take off, be able to de-orbit space debris actively, and mine the Moon or other celestial bodies – or even start settling on them.

What the specific needs for those future developments are in terms of law and regulation, to create both some sense of justice and some sense of predictability and foreseeability of human activity in or using outer space, is therefore very difficult to determine in any reasonable detail. Space lawyers, at the very least, should (continue to) follow developments in the technical, operational, political and commercial realms closely and make sure they understand their major aspects and elements, in order to ensure that understanding the legal requirements or consequences they would give rise to does not lag behind too far.

At a high level of abstraction, however, it is clear that outer space is, indeed, more and more becoming that fourth geographical realm, that final frontier for humankind to move into. As an increasing number of human activities that we have already become quite used to on Earth are now also becoming a reality, or at least a likelihood, in the context of outer space (whether this means actually undertaking such activities *in* outer space or rather *using* outer space as an instrument), it often boils down to transplanting relevant Earthbound legal regimes to a

---

484 See https://quoteinvestigator.com/2013/10/20/no-predict/ (last accessed 16 June 2020).

space setting while, of course, making sure that it is as necessary or desirable adapted or augmented to serve the specifics of that setting.

In each case, the Outer Space Treaty still will and indeed should guide and shape at least the initial developments. The absence of a legal possibility to claim territory in outer space, for instance, may be the ultimate bedrock of space law, and will continue to serve as the legal baseline for any specific legal regimes addressing space mining, space settlement, space debris mitigation, on-orbit servicing and a host of other, sometimes not yet fathomable developments in the real world. Concepts such as State responsibility and State liability will continue to drive national legislation to properly address the involvement of non-State actors – inevitable, and if properly bounded, generally beneficial to humankind's venturing deeper and deeper into outer space – and carefully balance its bona fide interests with the overarching interests of humankind as a whole, notably in terms of security, safety and the environment. Hopefully, experiences with developments in realms that have some similarity to outer space – the high seas, the airspaces, the Antarcticas of this world – will also allow us to avoid making certain mistakes again. Whether we like it or not, humankind depends upon its tiny blue marble of a planet, and we are all in this together; space law will continue to be an important tool in helping us to ensure 'Spaceship Earth' will be able to carry us much longer still.

Bibliography

Abbott, F.M., Intellectual Property, International Protection, in *The Max Planck Encyclopedia of Public International Law* (Ed. R. Wolfrum) *Vol. V* (2012).

Abeyratne, R., ICAO's Involvement in Outer Space Affairs – A Need for Closer Scrutiny, 30 *Journal of Space Law* (2004).

Baker, B., Hague Peace Conferences (1899 and 1907), in *The Max Planck Encyclopedia of Public International Law* (Ed. R. Wolfrum) *Vol. IV* (2012).

Balsano, A.M., & J. Wheeler, The IGA and ESA: Protecting Intellectual Property Rights in the Context of ISS Activities, in *The International Space Station* (Eds. F.G. von der Dunk & M.M.T.A. Brus) (2006).

Berlingheri, M., A Policy and Legal Framework for Commercial Utilisation, in *The International Space Station* (Eds. F.G. von der Dunk & M.M.T.A. Brus) (2006).

Bhagwati, J., Economic Perspective on Trade in Professional Services, in *Legal Problems of International Economic Relations* (Eds. J.H. Jackson, W.J. Davey & A.O. Sykes) (4th ed.) (2002).

Boas, G., *Public International Law* (2012).

Bohlmann, U.M., K.U. Schrogl & I. Zilioli, Report of the 'Project 2001' Working Group on Telecommunication, in *'Project 2001' – Legal Framework for the Commercial Use of Outer Space* (Ed. K.H. Böckstiegel) (2002).

Bohlmann, U.M., & G. Suess, Article XIII, in *Cologne Commentary on Space Law* (Eds. S. Hobe, B. Schmidt-Tedd & K.U. Schrogl) *Vol. I* (2009).

Brannen, T., Private Commercial Space Transportation's Dependence on Space Tourism and NASA's Responsibility to Both, 75 *Journal of Air Law and Commerce* (2010).

Brünner, C., & E. Walter (Eds.), *Nationales Weltraumrecht/National Space Law* (2008).

Cassese, A., *International Law* (2001).

Chaddha, S., U.S. Commercial Space Sector: Matured and Successful, 36 *Journal of Space Law* (2010).

Chatzipanagiotis, M., *The Legal Status of Space Tourists in the Framework of Commercial Suborbital Flights* (2011).

Cheng, B., *Studies in International Space Law* (1997).

Clarke, A.C., Extra-Terrestrial Relays, *Wireless World* (1945).

Cottier, T., Industrial Property, International Protection, in *The Max Planck Encyclopedia of Public International Law* (Ed. R. Wolfrum) *Vol. V* (2012).

Crawford, E., Geneva Conventions Additional Protocol I (1977), in *The Max Planck Encyclopedia of Public International Law* (Ed. R. Wolfrum) *Vol. IV* (2012).

Crawford, E., Geneva Conventions Additional Protocol II (1977), in *The Max Planck Encyclopedia of Public International Law* (Ed. R. Wolfrum) *Vol. IV* (2012).
Crawford, J., *Brownlie's Principles of Public International Law* (8th ed.) (2012).
Dembling, P.G., & D.M. Arons, The Evolution of the Outer Space Treaty, 33 *Journal of Air Law & Commerce* (1967).
Doldirina, C., Intellectual Property Rights in the Context of Space Activities, in *Handbook of Space Law* (Eds. F.G. von der Dunk & F. Tronchetti) (2015).
Farand, A., Jurisdiction and Liability Issues in Carrying out Commercial Activities in the International Space Station (ISS) Programme, in *The International Space Station* (Eds. F.G. von der Dunk & M.M.T.A. Brus) (2006).
Fernández de Casadevante Romani, C., Objective Regime, in *The Max Planck Encyclopedia of Public International Law* (Ed. R. Wolfrum) *Vol. VII* (2012).
Freeland, S.R., Fly Me to the Moon: How will International Law Cope with Commercial Space Tourism, 11 *Melbourne Journal of International Law* (2010).
Freeland, S.R., & R.S. Jakhu, Article II, in *Cologne Commentary on Space Law* (Eds. S. Hobe, B. Schmidt-Tedd & K.U. Schrogl) *Vol. I* (2009).
Frowein, J.A., Obligations *erga omnes*, in *The Max Planck Encyclopedia of Public International Law* (Ed. R. Wolfrum) *Vol. VII* (2012).
Gabrynowicz, J., *et al.*, The 1986 Principles Relating to Remote Sensing of the Earth from Outer Space, *Cologne Commentary on Space Law* (Eds. S. Hobe, B. Schmidt-Tedd & K.U. Schrogl) *Vol. III* (2015).
Gangale, T., *How High the Sky? The Definition and Delimitation of Outer Space and Territorial Airspace in International Law* (2019).
Gasser, H.P., & D. Thürer, Geneva Conventions I–IV (1949), in *The Max Planck Encyclopedia of Public International Law* (Ed. R. Wolfrum) *Vol. IV* (2012).
Gaubert, C., Insurance in the Context of Space Activities, in *Handbook of Space Law* (Eds. F.G. von der Dunk & F. Tronchetti) (2015).
Gerhard, M., Art. VI, in *Cologne Commentary on Space Law* (Eds. S. Hobe, B. Schmidt-Tedd & K.U. Schrogl) *Vol. I* (2009).
Gerhard, M., & K.U. Schrogl, Report of the 'Project 2001' Working Group on National Space Legislation, in *'Project 2001' – Legal Framework for the Commercial Use of Outer Space* (Ed. K.H. Böckstiegel) (2002).
Goh, G.M., Articles XIV–XVII, in *Cologne Commentary on Space Law* (Eds. S. Hobe, B. Schmidt-Tedd & K.U. Schrogl) *Vol. I* (2009).
Goh, G.M., *et al.*, The 1992 Principles Relevant to the Use of Nuclear Power Sources in Outer Space, in *Cologne Commentary on Space Law* (Eds. S. Hobe, B. Schmidt-Tedd & K.U. Schrogl) *Vol. III* (2015).
Gold, M.N., Lost in Space: A Practitioner's First-Hand Perspective on Reforming the U.S.'s Obsolete, Arrogant, and Counterproductive Export Control Regime for Space-Related Systems and Technologies, 34 *Journal of Space Law* (2008).
Harris, R., Science, Policy and Evidence in EO, in *Evidence from Earth Observation Satellites* (Eds. R. Purdy & D. Leung) (2013).
Henaku, B.D.K., *The Law on Global Air Navigation by Satellite: An Analysis of Legal Aspects of the ICAO CNS/ATM System* (1998).

Hobe, S., The Relevance of Current International Space Treaties in the 21st Century, 27 *Annals of Air and Space Law* (2002).
Hobe, S., Article I, in *Cologne Commentary on Space Law* (Eds. S. Hobe, B. Schmidt-Tedd & K.U. Schrogl) *Vol. I* (2009).
Hobe, S., Space Law – An Analysis of its Development and its Future, in *Outer Space in Society, Politics and Law* (Eds. C. Brünner & A. Soucek) (2011).
Hobe, S., et al., A New Chapter for Europe in Space, 54 *Zeitschrift für Luft- und Weltraumrecht* (2005).
Hobe, S., et al., The 1979 Agreement Governing the Activities of States on the Moon and Other Celestial Bodies, in *Cologne Commentary on Space Law* (Eds. S. Hobe, B. Schmidt-Tedd & K.U. Schrogl) *Vol. II* (2013).
Hobe, S., et al., The 1996 Declaration on International Cooperation in the Exploration and Use of Outer Space for the Benefit and in the Interest of all States, Taking into Particular Account the Needs of Developing Countries, in *Cologne Commentary on Space Law* (Eds. S. Hobe, B. Schmidt-Tedd & K.U. Schrogl) *Vol. III* (2015).
Hodgkins, K., Procedures for Return of Space Objects under the Agreement on the Rescue of Astronauts, the Return of Astronauts and the Return of Objects Launched into Outer Space, in *Proceedings United Nations/International Institute of Air and Space Law Workshop on Capacity Building in Space Law* (2003).
Hofmann, M., & A. Loukakis (Eds.), *Ownership of Satellites* (2017).
Hughes, T.R., & E. Rosenberg, Space Travel Law (and Politics): The Evolution of the Commercial Space Launch Amendments Act of 2004, 31 *Journal of Space Law* (2005).
Hurwitz, B.A., Reflections on the Cosmos 954 Incident, *Proceedings of the Thirty-Second Colloquium on the Law of Outer Space* (1990).
Hurwitz, B.A., *State Liability for Outer Space Activities in Accordance with the 1972 Convention on International Liability for Damage caused by Space Objects* (1992).
Hyman, W.A., *Magna Carta of Space* (1966).
Iavicoli, V., Italy and the Commercial Utilization of the International Space Station, in *The International Space Station* (Eds. F.G. von der Dunk & M.M.T.A. Brus) (2006).
Ito, A., *Legal Aspects of Satellite Remote Sensing* (2011).
Jankowitsch, P., The Role of the United Nations in Outer Space Law Development: Past Achievements and New Challenges, 26 *Journal of Space Law* (1998).
Jankowitsch, P., The Background and History of Space Law, in *Handbook of Space Law* (Eds. F.G. von der Dunk & F. Tronchetti) (2015).
Kadelbach, S., Nuclear Weapons and Warfare, in *The Max Planck Encyclopedia of Public International Law* (Ed. R. Wolfrum) *Vol. VII* (2012).
Kapustin, A., Article X, in *Cologne Commentary on Space Law* (Eds. S. Hobe, B. Schmidt-Tedd & K.U. Schrogl) *Vol. I* (2009).
Kerrest de Rozavel, A., & L.J. Smith, Article VII, in *Cologne Commentary on Space Law* (Eds. S. Hobe, B. Schmidt-Tedd & K.U. Schrogl) *Vol. I* (2009).
Kohlhase, C., & P.S. Makiol, Report of the 'Project 2001' Working Group on Launch and Associated Services, in *'Project 2001' – Legal Framework for the Commercial Use of Outer Space* (Ed. K.H. Böckstiegel) (2002).
Koplow, D.A., Exoatmospheric Plowshares: Using a Nuclear Explosive Device for

Planetary Defense Against an Incoming Asteroid, 23 *UCLA Journal of International Law and Foreign Affairs* (2019).

Köster, M., Legal Problems Related to a Combined Use of Airspace by Air- and Spacecraft, in *'Project 2001' – Legal Framework for the Commercial Use of Outer Space* (Ed. K.H. Böckstiegel) (2002).

Lachs, M., *The Law of Outer Space* (reprint 2010).

Lafferranderie, G., Introduction, in *Outlook on Space Law over the Next 30 Years* (Eds. G. Lafferranderie & D. Crowther) (1997).

Lee, Y., Registration of Space Objects: ESA Member States' Practice, 22 *Space Policy* (2006).

Ley, W., & W. Stoffel, Report of the 'Project 2001' Working Group on Space Stations, in *'Project 2001' – Legal Framework for the Commercial Use of Outer Space* (Ed. K.H. Böckstiegel) (2002).

Lyall, F., On the Reform of the ITU and the Commercial Use of Space, in *'Project 2001' – Legal Framework for the Commercial Use of Outer Space* (Ed. K.H. Böckstiegel) (2002).

Lyall, F., *International Communications – The International Telecommunication Union and Universal Postal Union* (2011).

Lyall, F., INMARSAT, in *The Max Planck Encyclopedia of Public International Law* (Ed. R. Wolfrum) *Vol. V* (2012).

Lyall, F., & P.B. Larsen, *Space Law – A Treatise* (2009).

Malanczuk, P., Space Law as a Branch of International Law, 25 *Netherlands International Law Yearbook* (1994).

Marboe, I., J. Neumann & K.U. Schrogl, The 1968 Agreement on the Rescue of Astronauts, the Return of Astronauts and the Return of Objects Launched into Outer Space, in *Cologne Commentary on Space Law* (Eds. S. Hobe, B. Schmidt-Tedd & K.U. Schrogl) *Vol. II* (2013).

Marboe, I., National Space Law, in *Handbook of Space Law* (Eds. F.G. von der Dunk & F. Tronchetti) (2015).

Marboe, I., S. Aoki & T. Brisibe, The 2013 Resolution on Recommendations on National Space Legislation Relevant to the Peaceful Exploration and Use of Outer Space, in *Cologne Commentary on Space Law* (Eds. S. Hobe, B. Schmidt-Tedd & K.U. Schrogl) *Vol. III* (2015).

Marchisio, S., Remote Sensing for Sustainable Development in International Law, in *Outlook on Space Law over the Next 30 Years* (Eds. G. Lafferranderie & D. Crowther) (1997).

Marchisio, S., Article IX, in *Cologne Commentary on Space Law* (Eds. S. Hobe, B. Schmidt-Tedd & K.U. Schrogl) *Vol. I* (2009).

Marsoof, A., A Case for *Sui Generis* Treatment of Software under the WTO Regime, 20 *International Journal of Law and Information Technology* (2012).

Mayence, J.F., Harmful Interference in Telecommunications under International and National Space Law, in *Harmful Interference in Regulatory Perspective* (Ed. M. Hofmann) (2015).

Mayence, J.F., & T. Reuter, Article XI, in *Cologne Commentary on Space Law* (Eds. S. Hobe, B. Schmidt-Tedd & K.U. Schrogl) *Vol. I* (2009).

McCormick, P.K., Neo-Liberalism: A Contextual Framework for Assessing the Privatisation of Intergovernmental Satellite Organisations, in *The Transformation of Intergovernmental Satellite Organisations* (Eds. P.K. McCormick & M.J. Mechanick) (2013).

McCormick, P.K., Intelsat: Pre- and Post-Private Equity Ownership, in *The Transformation of Intergovernmental Satellite Organisations* (Eds. P.K. McCormick & M.J. Mechanick) (2013).

Mechanick, M.J., The Role and Function of Residual International Intergovernmental Satellite Organisations Following Privatisation, in *The Transformation of Intergovernmental Satellite Organisations* (Eds. P.K. McCormick & M.J. Mechanick) (2013).

Meredith, P.L., & S.P. Fleming, U.S. Space Technology Exports: The Current Political Climate, 27 *Journal of Space Law* (1999).

Perlman, B., Grounding U.S. Commercial Space Regulation in the Constitution, 100 *The Georgetown Law Journal* (2012).

Ramey, R.A., Armed Conflict on the Final Frontier: The Law of War in Space, 48 *Air Force Law Review* (2000).

Rathgeber, W., N.L. Remuss & K.U. Schrogl, Space Security and the European Code of Conduct for Outer Space Activities, 4 *Disarmament Forum* (2009).

Reif, S.U., B. Schmidt-Tedd & K. Wannenmacher, Report of the 'Project 2001' Working Group on Privatisation, in *'Project 2001' – Legal Framework for the Commercial Use of Outer Space* (Ed. K.H. Böckstiegel) (2002).

Ribbelink, O., Article III, in *Cologne Commentary on Space Law* (Eds. S. Hobe, B. Schmidt-Tedd & K.U. Schrogl) *Vol. I* (2009).

Rosmalen, S., The International Space Station Past, Present and Future – An Overview, in *The International Space Station* (Eds. F.G. von der Dunk & M.M.T.A. Brus) (2006).

Sagar, D., Privatization of the International Satellite Organizations, in *'Project 2001' – Legal Framework for the Commercial Use of Outer Space* (Ed. K.H. Böckstiegel) (2002).

Sagar, D., & P.K. McCormick, Inmarsat: In the Forefront of Mobile Satellite Communications, in *The Transformation of Intergovernmental Satellite Organisations* (Eds. P.K. McCormick & M.J. Mechanick) (2013).

Sánchez Aranzamendi, M., F. Riemann & K.U. Schrogl, The 2004 Resolution on the Application of the Concept of the 'Launching State', in *Cologne Commentary on Space Law* (Eds. S. Hobe, B. Schmidt-Tedd & K.U. Schrogl) *Vol. III* (2015).

Schaefer, M.P., Analogues Between Space Law and Law of the Sea/International Maritime Law: Can Space Law Usefully Borrow or Adapt Rules from these Other Areas of Public International Law?, in *2012 Proceedings of the International Institute of Space Law* (2013).

Schindler, D., & J. Toman, *The Laws of Armed Conflicts* (1988).

Schmidt-Tedd, B., & S. Mick, Article VIII, in *Cologne Commentary on Space Law* (Eds. S. Hobe, B. Schmidt-Tedd & K.U. Schrogl) *Vol. I* (2009).

Schmidt-Tedd, B., et al., The 1975 Convention on Registration of Objects Launched into Outer Space, in *Cologne Commentary on Space Law* (Eds. S. Hobe, B. Schmidt-Tedd & K.U. Schrogl) *Vol. II* (2013).

Schmidt-Tedd, B., N. Hedman & A.M. Hurtz, The 2007 Resolution on Recommendations on Enhancing the Practice of States and International Intergovernmental Organizations in Registering Space Objects, in *Cologne Commentary on Space Law* (Eds. S. Hobe, B. Schmidt-Tedd & K.U. Schrogl) *Vol. III* (2015).

Schrogl, K.U., & J. Neumann, Article IV, in *Cologne Commentary on Space Law* (Eds. S. Hobe, B. Schmidt-Tedd & K.U. Schrogl) *Vol. I* (2009).

Sharpe, C., & F. Tronchetti, Legal Aspects of Public Manned Spaceflight, in *Handbook of Space Law* (Eds. F.G. von der Dunk) (2015).

Shaw, M.A., *International Law* (4th ed.) (1997).

Smith, L.J., Legal Aspects of Commercial Utilization of the International Space Station: A German Perspective, in *The International Space Station* (Eds. F.G. von der Dunk & M.M.T.A. Brus) (2006).

Smith, L.J., A. Kerrest de Rozavel & F. Tronchetti, The 1972 Convention on International Liability for Damage Caused by Space Objects, in *Cologne Commentary on Space Law* (Eds. S. Hobe, B. Schmidt-Tedd & K.U. Schrogl) *Vol. II* (2013).

Soucek, A., International Law, in *Outer Space in Society, Politics and Law* (Eds. C. Brünner & A. Soucek) (2011).

Stoll, P.T., World Trade Organization (WTO), in *The Max Planck Encyclopedia of Public International Law* (Ed. R. Wolfrum) *Vol. X* (2012).

Strydom, H.A., Weapons of Mass Destruction, in *The Max Planck Encyclopedia of Public International Law* (Ed. R. Wolfrum) *Vol. X* (2012).

Stubbe, P., M. Ferrazzani & O. Huth, The 1982 Principles Governing the Use by States of Artificial Earth Satellites for International Direct Television Broadcasting, in *Cologne Commentary on Space Law* (Eds. S. Hobe, B. Schmidt-Tedd & K.U. Schrogl) *Vol. III* (2015).

Stubbe, P., et al., The 2007 Space Debris Mitigation Guidelines of the Committee on the Peaceful Uses of Outer Space, in *Cologne Commentary on Space Law* (Eds. S. Hobe, B. Schmidt-Tedd & K.U. Schrogl) *Vol. III* (2015).

Sundahl, M.J., The Duty to Rescue Space Tourists and Return Private Spacecraft, 35 *Journal of Space Law* (2009).

Sundahl, M.J., Financing Space Ventures, in *Handbook of Space Law* (Eds. F.G. von der Dunk & F. Tronchetti) (2015).

Thirlway, H., The Sources of International Law, in *International Law* (Ed. M.D. Evans) (2003).

Tomas, L., Air Law, in *The Max Planck Encyclopedia of Public International Law* (Ed. R. Wolfrum) *Vol. I* (2012).

Treves, T., Customary International Law, in *The Max Planck Encyclopedia of Public International Law* (Ed. R. Wolfrum) *Vol. II* (2012).

Tronchetti, F., *The Exploitation of Natural Resources of the Moon and Other Celestial Bodies* (2009).

Tronchetti, F., Legal Aspects of the Military Uses of Outer Space, in *Handbook of Space Law* (Eds. F.G. von der Dunk & F. Tronchetti) (2015).

Tronchetti, F., Legal Aspects of Satellite Remote Sensing, in *Handbook of Space Law* (Eds. F.G. von der Dunk & F. Tronchetti) (2015).

Van Fenema, P., Suborbital Flights and ICAO, 30 *Air and Space Law* (2005).

Van Fenema, P., Legal Aspects of Launch Services and Space Transportation, in *Handbook of Space Law* (Eds. F.G. von der Dunk & F. Tronchetti) (2015).

Veldhuyzen, R.P., & T.L. Masson-Zwaan, ESA Policy and Impending Legal Framework for Commercial Utilisation of the European Columbus Laboratory Module of the ISS, in *The International Space Station* (Eds. F.G. von der Dunk & M.M.T.A. Brus) (2006).

Vereshchetin, V.S., & G.M. Danilenko, Custom as a Source of International Law of Outer Space, 13 *Journal of Space Law* (1985).

Viikari, L., Environmental Aspects of Space Activities, in *Handbook of Space Law* (Eds. F.G. von der Dunk & F. Tronchetti) (2015).

Vissepó, V.J., Legal Aspects of Reusable Launch Vehicles, 31 *Journal of Space Law* (2005).

Von der Dunk, F.G., Liability versus Responsibility in Space Law: Misconception or Misconstruction?, in *Proceedings of the Thirty-Fourth Colloquium on the Law of Outer Space* (1992).

Von der Dunk, F.G., *Private Enterprise and Public Interest in the European 'Spacescape'* (1997).

Von der Dunk, F.G., Non-Discriminatory Data Dissemination in Practice, in *Earth Observation Data Policy and Europe* (Ed. R. Harris) (2002).

Von der Dunk, F.G., The Registration Convention: Background and Historical Context, in *Proceedings of the Forty-Sixth Colloquium on the Law of Outer Space* (2003).

Von der Dunk, F.G., A European 'Equivalent' to United States Export Controls: European Law on the Control of International Trade in Dual-Use Space Technologies, 7 *Astropolitics* (2009).

Von der Dunk, F.G., Surveying the Scene: The Effects of Globalisation on Space Law – A Panelist's Remarks, in *Globalisation – The State and International Law* (Ed. S. Hobe) (2009).

Von der Dunk, F.G. (Ed.), *National Space Legislation in Europe* (2011).

Von der Dunk, F.G., The EU Space Competence as per the Treaty of Lisbon: Sea Change or Empty Shell?, in *Proceedings of the International Institute of Space Law 2011* (2012).

Von der Dunk, F.G., Crossing a Rubycon? The International Legal Framework for ISOs – Before and After Privatisation, in *The Transformation of Intergovernmental Satellite Organisations* (Eds. P.K. McCormick & M.J. Mechanick) (2013).

Von der Dunk, F.G., Cutting the Bread, 29 *Space Policy* (2013).

Von der Dunk, F.G., Towards 'Flags of Convenience' in Space?, in *Proceedings of the International Institute of Space Law 2012* (2013).

Von der Dunk, F.G., Beyond *What*? Beyond *Earth Orbit*? …! The Applicability of the Registration Convention to Private Commercial Manned Sub-Orbital Spaceflight, 43 *California Western International Law Journal* (2013).

Von der Dunk, F.G., Federal *versus* State: Private Commercial Spaceflight Operator Immunity Regulation in the United States, in *Proceedings of the International Institute of Space Law 2013* (IISL) (2014).

Von der Dunk, F.G., Preface, in *Handbook of Space Law* (Eds. F.G. von der Dunk & F. Tronchetti) (2015).

Von der Dunk, F.G., International Space Law, in *Handbook of Space Law* (Eds. F.G. von der Dunk & F. Tronchetti) (2015).

Von der Dunk, F.G., European Space Law, in *Handbook of Space Law* (Eds. F.G. von der Dunk & F. Tronchetti) (2015).

Von der Dunk, F.G., International Organizations in Space Law, in *Handbook of Space Law* (Eds. F.G. von der Dunk & F. Tronchetti) (2015).

Von der Dunk, F.G., Legal Aspects of Satellite Communications, in *Handbook of Space Law* (Eds. F.G. von der Dunk & F. Tronchetti) (2015).

Von der Dunk, F.G., Legal Aspects of Private Manned Spaceflight, in *Handbook of Space Law* (Eds. F.G. von der Dunk & F. Tronchetti) (2015).

Von der Dunk, F.G., International Trade Aspects of Space Services, in *Handbook of Space Law* (Eds. F.G. von der Dunk & F. Tronchetti) (2015).

Von der Dunk, F.G., Space Traffic Management: A Challenge of Cosmic Proportions, in *Proceedings of the International Institute of Space Law 2015* (IISL) (2016).

Von der Dunk, F.G., *Citius, Altius, Fortius* – Regulating Commercial Spaceflight under Air Law or Space Law?, in *Harmonising Regulatory and Antitrust Regimes for International Air Transport* (Ed. J. Walulik) (2019).

Von der Dunk, F.G., Scoping National Space Law: The True Meaning of 'National Activities in Outer Space' of Article VI of the Outer Space Treaty, to be published in *Proceedings of the International Institute of Space Law 2019* (2020).

Von der Dunk, F.G., & G.M. Goh, Article V, in *Cologne Commentary on Space Law* (Eds. S. Hobe, B. Schmidt-Tedd & K.U. Schrogl) *Vol. I* (2009).

Von Heinegg, W.H., Neutrality and Outer Space, 93 *International Law Studies* (2017).

Vöneky, S., & S. Addison-Agyei, Antarctica, in *The Max Planck Encyclopedia of Public International Law* (Ed. R. Wolfrum) *Vol. I* (2012).

Waldrop, E.S., Integration of Military and Civilian Space Assets: Legal and National Security Implications, 55 *Air Force Law Review* (2004).

Westphal, D., International Telecommunication Union (ITU), in *The Max Planck Encyclopedia of Public International Law* (Ed. R. Wolfrum) *Vol. VI* (2012).

Williams, M., The UN Principles on Remote Sensing Today, in *Proceedings of the Forty-Eighth Colloquium on the Law of Outer Space* (2006).

Williamson, R.A., Legal and Policy Issues in Satellite Remote Sensing, in *'Project 2001' – Legal Framework for the Commercial Use of Outer Space* (Ed. K.H. Böckstiegel) (2002).

Wolfrüm, R., & J. Pichon, Consensus, in *The Max Planck Encyclopedia of Public International Law* (Ed. R. Wolfrum) *Vol. II* (2012).

Index

ABM Treaty (1972) 75
Agreement on Basic Telecommunication 110
aircraft 100, 102, 103, 107
air law 99–108
airline industry 101–102
airspace 107
Aldrin, Buzz 114
Antarctic Treaty (1959) 8
    Consultative Parties 8
Apollo Moon landers 114
Argentina 111, 116, 122
Argentine Decree creating CONAE (1991) 115
Arms Export Control Act 86
Armstrong, Neil 114
astronauts *vs.* spaceflight participants 26–7
Australia 49, 56, 111, 121
Austria 120

ballistic missile proliferation 75
baseline liability regime 29, 30
battlefields 77
Belgium 119
Benefits Declaration (1996) 16
Berne Convention (1886) 95
bilateral agreements 42, 75
Brazil 63, 111, 121

Canada 32, 44, 45, 49, 111, 121
Canadian territory 32
Cape Town Convention 90
CCL *see* US Commerce Control List
celestial bodies 56, 57
Centre National d'Etudes Spatiales 115

CGEA *see* Community General Export Authorization
Chicago Convention (1944) 99, 105
China 63, 74, 82, 111, 116, 122
Claims Commission 33
    modus operandi of 31
classical aviation 101
CNES *see* Centre National d'Etudes Spatiales
Cold War 18, 44, 96
commercialization process 49
commercial manned spaceflight regulation 105–106
Commercial Space Act (1998) 104, 119
commercial spaceflight 101
    air law-approach 103
    basis of international space law 108
    private 102, 103, 106
    rules for 106
Commercial Space Launch Act 104
    section 50914(b)(1) of 105
Commercial Space Launch Amendments Act (2004) 105
Commercial Space Launch Competitiveness Act (2015) 105, 119
Committee on the Peaceful Uses of Outer Space (COPUOS) 14, 38, 39, 72
common heritage of mankind principle 55, 58
Communications Act (1934) 118
Community General Export Authorization (CGEA) 88
Comprehensive Test Ban Treaty (1996) 74
controlled (national) airspace 106
Convention Concerning the Protection of the World Cultural and Natural Heritage 114

137

Convention concerning the Rights and Duties of Neutral Powers in Naval War 77
Convention relative to the Rights and Duties of Neutral Powers and Persons in Case of War on Land 77
COPUOS *see* Committee on the Peaceful Uses of Outer Space
copyright(s)
 and neighbouring rights 98
 protection 96
 regimes 94, 95
 space 93
copyright law 97
corpus iuris spatialis internationalis 8, 13, 14, 64, 73, 76, 79, 81, 91, 106, 108, 114
 core body of 41
 definition of 39–40
 Geneva system *vs.* 77
 inner core of 39–40, 75, 118
Cosmos-954 case 31–2
crew *vs.* spaceflight participants 27
criminal air law applications 100, 107
customary international law 14, 39–40, 59–63
 on space debris 80

Database Directive (1996) 97
Declaration on Principles (1963) 15
Denmark 120
Draft International Code of Conduct for Outer Space Activities 83
Draft Treaty on the Prevention of the Placement of Weapons in Outer Space 82
dual-use space technologies 83–9

EASA *see* European Aviation Safety Agency
EEC *see* European Economic Community
ENMOD Convention (1977) 74
Europe 49, 103, 108
European Aviation Safety Agency (EASA) 103
European-continental approach 97
European Economic Community (EEC) 113

European Space Agency (ESA) Convention 12, 51–4, 98
 categories of activities 52
 geographical distribution/fair return clause 53
 industrial policy principle 53
 legal framework 52
 optional activities 52
 purpose of 51–2
European Space Agency (ESA) Council 52
European Union 83, 87, 88, 97, 111, 113
European Union Database Directive 97
EUTELSAT 48
Export Administration Act 87
Export Administration Regulations 87

fall-back clause 19
Federal Aviation Authority 104
Finland 120
first ring of space law *see* Northern part of first ring of space law; Southern part of first ring of space law
fixed satellite services 47
flag of convenience 124, 125
Fourth Protocol to the GATS (1997) 110
France 54, 74, 120
freedom of scientific investigation 3
French Statute establishing CNES (1961) 115

GATS *see* General Agreement on Trade in Services
General Agreement on Tariffs and Trade (1947) 109
General Agreement on Trade in Services (GATS) 109, 111, 112
 Annex on Telecommunications 109
general international law approach 20
Geneva system 76
Geographic Information Systems (GIS) 96
Germany 54, 98, 116, 121
GIS *see* Geographic Information Systems
Global Maritime Distress and Safety System (GMDSS) 50–51
GMDSS *see* Global Maritime Distress and Safety System
Greece 120

Hague Peace Conference (1899) 77
Hague Peace Conference (1907) 77
Hague system 77
Hong Kong 120

IADC *see* Inter-Agency Space Debris Consultation Committee
ICAO *see* International Civil Aviation Organization
ICOC *see* International Code of Conduct
IGOs *see* intergovernmental organizations
IMSO *see* International Mobile Satellite Organisation
India 63, 74, 111, 122
Indian ASAT test 39
Indonesia 111, 120
INMARSAT 47–50, 108
   Convention 48
   Operating Agreement 48
intellectual property rights 46, 94–8
   as concept 94
   copyright protection 96
   copyright regimes 94, 95
   copyrights and neighbouring rights 98
   European-continental approach 97
   first-to-file 98
   first-to-invent 98
   patent rights 94–5
   protection and enforcement 95
   utilitarian Anglo-American approach 96–7
INTELSAT 47–50, 108
INTELSAT Operating Agreement 48
Inter-Agency Space Debris Consultation Committee (IADC) 38, 39, 54
Intergovernmental Agreement on International Space Station 11, 44–7
   criminal jurisdiction 46
   intellectual property rights 46
   Protected Space Operations 46–7
   retain jurisdiction 45
   rules of international space law regime 46
   Space Age 47

Intergovernmental Agreement on ISS 11, 98
intergovernmental organizations (IGOs) 50
International Civil Aviation Organization (ICAO) 103
International Code of Conduct (ICOC)
   against ballistic missile proliferation 75
   Draft for Outer Space Activities 83
international cooperation 21
International Court of Justice 7
international humanitarian law 76, 78
International Institute for the Unification of Private Law 89
international law on military activities and operations 72–83
international liability regime 121
International Mobile Satellite Organisation (IMSO)
   Convention 11, 44, 55, 64
   Public Service Agreement 50
international regimes
   dual-use space technologies 83–9
   international use of radio frequencies 67–72
international satellite organizations 108
international space law 4, 8, 66, 116–17, 125
International Space Station (ISS) 26
International Telecommunication Satellite Organisation (ITSO) 50
   Agreement 11, 47–51
   Convention 47–51
   Public Service Agreement 50
International Telecommunication Union (ITU) 68, 90
International Telegraph Union (ITU) 68
international trade law 125
International Traffic in Arms Regulations (ITARs) 86
ISS *see* International Space Station
Italy 54, 98, 116, 122
ITARs *see* International Traffic in Arms Regulations
ITSO *see* International Telecommunication Satellite Organisation

ITU *see* International Telecommunication Union; International Telegraph Union
ius ad bellum 76, 78
ius in bello 76

Jacobs, D.L. 1
Japan 44, 49, 111, 120

Kazakhstan 120

launching authority 26, 27, 28
launching State 30, 34, 38, 123, 125
Launching State Resolution (2004) 16, 123–4
Law establishing the Brazilian space agency (1994) 116
law of armed conflict 76, 80, 82
lex generalis 114
  of international law 66, 73, 79
  of space law 9
lex posterior 72
lex specialis 72, 73, 79, 80, 114
  of space law 5, 9, 41, 66
  of the Treaty 19
lex specialis derogat lege generalis 19
Liability Convention (1972) 5, 9, 10, 14, 16, 28–33, 37, 44, 46, 54, 81, 108, 116, 122–5
licensing private space operators 39
Lifeline Connectivity 51
Lifeline Connectivity Obligations 50
Lisbon Treaty (2007) 113
London 50
Lotus principle 6
Lotus, SS 4
Low-Earth Orbit 44
Luxembourg 57, 58, 121

Magna Carta 6
Master International Frequency Register 71
materiae personae 123
Mexico 111, 122
military activities and operations, international law on 72–83

Missile Technology Control Regime (MTCR) 84–7
  Equipment, Software, and Technology Annex 84
  Guidelines for Sensitive Missile-relevant Transfers 84
mobile satellite services 47
modus operandi of Claims Commission 31
Montreal Convention (1999) 100
Moon Agreement (1969) 10–11, 15, 40, 54–8
Most-Favoured-Nation (MFN) principles 109
MTCR *see* Missile Technology Control Regime
multilateral treaties 42–3

NASA *see* National Aeronautics and Space Administration
National Aeronautics and Space Administration (NASA) 86, 115
national registration obligations 36
national space law 116–17
national space legislation 9, 13
  components of 115
  overview of 115–17
  private sector space activities 117–21
  scope and approach of 121–4
  see also space law
National Space Legislation Resolution (2013) 16, 122, 123
National Treatment (NT) 109, 110
Netherlands, the 119
NewSpace 89
New York Times 1
New Zealand 121
Nigeria 111, 120
Non-Proliferation Treaty (1968) 84
Northern part of first ring of space law bilateral agreements 42
  customary international law 59–63
  ESA Convention 51–4
  Intergovernmental Agreement on International Space Station 44–7
  ITSO Agreement 47–51
  IMSO Convention 47–51
  Moon Agreement 54–8

multilateral treaties 42–3
overview of 42–4
space mining 54–8
UN Principles on Remote Sensing 59–63
see also space law
North Korea 74
Norway 121
NT *see* National Treatment

OCST *see* Office for Commercial Space Transportation
Office for Commercial Space Transportation (OCST) 104
Office of the Associate Administrator for Commercial Space Transportation 104
OrionSat 109
outer space
  description of 1–2
  exploration and use of 3
  global commons character of 18
  in Lotus case 4
  Magna Carta 6
Outer Space Treaty 9, 10, 12, 14, 44, 127
  all-encompassing nature of 40
  Article I of 16, 18, 19, 47, 49, 50, 57, 58, 60
  Article II of 16, 19, 58, 97, 100, 108
  Article III of 17, 18–19, 21, 48, 59, 66, 73
  Article IV of 20, 36, 58, 73
  Article V of 23, 25
  Article VI of 17, 18, 23, 24, 28, 30, 61, 71, 108, 118, 122
  Article VII of 17, 18, 24, 28, 29, 33, 46, 108, 118, 122–4
  Article VIII of 5, 17, 18, 23, 25, 31, 33, 35, 37, 45, 97
  Article IX of 21
  Article X of 20, 73
  Article XI of 20, 73
  Article XIII of 28
  fundamental character and importance of 4
  general international law 5
  general provisions of 55

humans in outer space 23
inanimate objects 23
international cooperation 21
legal value of structural provisions of 6–8
Lotus principle 6
non-governmental entities 24
scientific aspects of space activities 22–3
space law in 3
space law *stricto sensu* 16–25
State's liability for international damage 5
substantive regime 18

PanAmSat 109
Paris Convention (1883) 95
Paris Convention (1919) 99
Partial Test Ban Treaty (1963) 12, 73
patent law 98
patent legislation 97
patent rights 94–5
Patents in Outer Space Act (1990) 97
Portugal 120
Principles on Direct Broadcasting by Satellite (1982) 15, 98
Principles on Nuclear Power Sources (1992) 15, 32
Principles Treaty 25
private air law 100
private commercial spaceflight 102–104, 106, 107
private human spaceflight 107
private manned spaceflight 99–108
private remote sensing satellite operators 119
private sector space activities 117–21
private sub-orbital flight 101
privatization process 49, 50
Protected Space Operations (PSOs) 46
Protocol (1974) 75
PSOs *see* Protected Space Operations
PTOs *see* Public Telecommunication Operators
Public Service Agreement
  IMSO 50
  ITSO 50

Public Service Obligations 50
Public Telecommunication Operators (PTOs) 48, 49

quasi-territorial criterion 46
quasi-territorial jurisdiction 5

radio-controlled spacecraft 2
radio frequencies, international use of 67–72
  allocation/reservation 70, 71
  assignment 71
  ITU system 68
  Master International Frequency Register 71
  Radio Regulations 70
  satellite communications 69
  Table of Frequency Allocations 70
  telemetry, tracking and control (TT&C) operations 68
Radio Regulations 69, 70
ratione materiae 47, 88, 122
ratione personae 47, 88
regional space law 120
Registration Convention (1975) 6, 10, 14, 16, 33–7, 38, 44, 53, 80, 108
  Article VII of 45
Registration Practice Resolution (2007) 16, 35
remote sensing *see* UN Principles on Remote Sensing (1986)
reparation 28
Rescue Agreement (1968) 10, 14, 25–8, 37, 44, 54, 80, 108
reusable launch vehicles (RLVs) 105
RLVs *see* reusable launch vehicles
Russia 44, 74, 82, 111, 119

SARPs *see* Standards and Recommended Practices
satellite communication 69
satellite communication services 108–12
Scaled Composites of 2004 X-Prize 101
Schedule of Specific Commitments
  application of NT 110
  service provision complexity of 111

second ring of space law
  air law 99–108
  intellectual property rights 94–8
  international law regimes 92
  international trade law 93
  overview of 92–3
  private manned spaceflight 99–108
  satellite communication services 108–12
  space copyrights 93
  space tourism 99–108
  see also space law
SES Astra 108
soft-law set of principles 36
South Africa 111, 119
Southern part of first ring of space law
  international law on military activities and operations 72–83
  international use of radio frequencies 67–72
  overview of 66–7
  sensitive dual-use space technologies 83–9
  see also space law
South Korea 111, 121
sovereignty 3, 57, 59–60, 78, 86, 99, 100, 108, 124
Soviet cosmonauts 21
Soviet Union 21, 32, 44, 75, 126
Space Age 21, 47, 75, 101
Space Assets Protocol 90
space copyrights 93
space customary international law 7–9
space debris 37–9
  customary international law 80
  Space Debris Mitigation Guidelines 38
  Space Debris Mitigation Guidelines of the Committee on the Peaceful Uses of Outer Space 38–9
spaceflight operators 105
spaceflight participants
  astronauts *vs.* 26–7
  crew *vs.* 27
space law
  activities 1–2
  defining 1

first ring of *see* Northern part of first ring of space law; Southern part of first ring of space law
  future of 126–7
  international 4, 8, 66, 116–17, 125
  national 116–17
  regional 120
  second ring of 92–114
  space-characteristics 1
  structure of 3–6
  substance of 8–10
  third ring of *see* national space legislation
space law *largo sensu* 9, 10, 11, 115
space law *lato sensu* 112
space law *stricto sensu* 8, 9
  Liability Convention (1972) 28–33
  Outer Space Treaty 16–25
  overview of 14–16
  Registration Convention (1975) 33–7
  Rescue Agreement (1968) 25–8
  space customary international law 37–9
  space debris 37–9
space mining 25, 54–8
space objects 100, 124–5
Spaceship Earth 127
space tourism 26, 99–108
Spain 116, 122
Sputnik-1 68
Standards and Recommended Practices (SARPs) 103
State liability 5, 18, 118, 125, 127
State Party to the Treaty 4, 18, 24
State responsibility 17, 18, 58, 108, 118, 127
Statute establishing the Russian space agency (1992) 115–16
Strategic Defense Initiative 20
sub-orbital flights 103, 104, 105
sub-orbital point-to-point transportation 106
sui generis intellectual property right 97
Sweden 119

Table of Frequency Allocations 70
telemetry, tracking and control (TT&C) operations 68

terrestrial international law 73
territorial jurisdiction 2
territorial sovereignty 3, 19
third ring of space law *see* national space legislation
Tokyo Convention (1963) 100, 107
two-pronged approach 33

Ukraine 119
UN Charter 12, 19, 21, 41, 73, 78, 81, 91
UN General Assembly Declarations 59
UN General Assembly Resolutions 14, 15
UNIDROIT 89
United Arab Emirates 57, 58, 120
United Kingdom 54, 119
United Nations 14, 72, 78, 81, 124
United Nations Convention on the Law of the Sea (1982) 55–7
United States 21, 27, 44, 49, 57, 58, 74, 75, 86, 97, 98, 103, 104, 105, 109, 111, 118, 122
UNOOSA *see* UN's Office of Outer Space Affairs
UN Principles on Remote Sensing (1986) 15, 59–63
  access on non-discriminatory basis 61–3
  analysed information 61–2
  cardinal clause of the Principles 61
  primary data definition of 61
  processed data definition of 61
  right of prior consent 60
UN Resolutions 40
UN Secretary General 22, 26, 34, 37
UN Security Council 79
UN Security Council-ordered/mandated military operations 19
UN's Office of Outer Space Affairs (UNOOSA) 34
US air law 105
US Commerce Control List (CCL) 87
US Department of State 86, 87
USML *see* US Munitions List
US Munitions List (USML) 86, 87
US National Aeronautics and Space Act (1958) 115
US patent law 98

US Patents in Space Act 98
US-registered spacecraft 97–8
utilitarian Anglo-American approach 96–7

Virgin Galactic, case study 102

WARC *see* World Radio Administrative Conference, 1959
Wassenaar Arrangement (1995) 84–5
weapons of mass destruction 20, 82
WIPO *see* World Intellectual Property Organization

WIPO Convention (1967) 96
Woomera Manual on the International Law of Military Space Operations 79
World Intellectual Property Organization (WIPO) 96
World Radio Administrative Conference, 1959 (WARC) 68
World Radio Conferences 70
World Trade Organization (WTO) 12, 109, 112
WTO *see* World Trade Organization
WTO Reference Paper 111

Titles in the **Elgar Advanced Introductions** series include:

International Political Economy
Benjamin J. Cohen

The Austrian School of Economics
Randall G. Holcombe

Cultural Economics
Ruth Towse

Law and Development
Michael J. Trebilcock and Mariana Mota Prado

International Humanitarian Law
Robert Kolb

International Trade Law
Michael J. Trebilcock

Post Keynesian Economics
J.E. King

International Intellectual Property
Susy Frankel and Daniel J. Gervais

Public Management and Administration
Christopher Pollitt

Organised Crime
Leslie Holmes

Nationalism
Liah Greenfeld

Social Policy
Daniel Béland and Rianne Mahon

Globalisation
Jonathan Michie

Entrepreneurial Finance
Hans Landström

International Conflict and Security Law
Nigel D. White

Comparative Constitutional Law
Mark Tushnet

International Human Rights Law
Dinah L. Shelton

Entrepreneurship
Robert D. Hisrich

International Tax Law
Reuven S. Avi-Yonah

Public Policy
B. Guy Peters

The Law of International Organizations
Jan Klabbers

International Environmental Law
Ellen Hey

International Sales Law
Clayton P. Gillette

Corporate Venturing
Robert D. Hisrich

Public Choice
Randall G. Holcombe

Private Law
Jan M. Smits

Consumer Behavior Analysis
Gordon Foxall

Behavioral Economics
John F. Tomer

Cost-Benefit Analysis
Robert J. Brent

Environmental Impact Assessment
Angus Morrison-Saunders

Comparative Constitutional Law
Second Edition
Mark Tushnet

National Innovation Systems
Cristina Chaminade, Bengt-Åke Lundvall and Shagufta Haneef

Ecological Economics
Matthias Ruth

Private International Law and Procedure
Peter Hay

Freedom of Expression
Mark Tushnet

Law and Globalisation
Jaakko Husa

Regional Innovation Systems
Bjørn T. Asheim, Arne Isaksen and Michaela Trippl

International Political Economy
Second Edition
Benjamin J. Cohen

International Tax Law
Second Edition
Reuven S. Avi-Yonah

Social Innovation
Frank Moulaert and Diana MacCallum

The Creative City
Charles Landry

International Trade Law
Michael J. Trebilcock and Joel Trachtman

European Union Law
Jacques Ziller

Planning Theory
Robert A. Beauregard

Tourism Destination Management
Chris Ryan

International Investment Law
August Reinisch

Sustainable Tourism
David Weaver

Austrian School of Economics
Second Edition
Randall G. Holcombe

U.S. Criminal Procedure
Christopher Slobogin

Platform Economics
Robin Mansell and W. Edward Steinmueller

Public Finance
Vito Tanzi

Feminist Economics
Joyce P. Jacobsen

Human Dignity and Law
James R. May and Erin Daly

Space Law
Frans G. von der Dunk

Elgar Advanced Introductions are stimulating and thoughtful introductions to major fields in the social sciences and law, expertly written by the world's leading scholars. Designed to be accessible yet rigorous, they offer concise and lucid surveys of the substantive and policy issues associated with discrete subject areas.

Frans G. von der Dunk, a leading authority on space law, presents a nuanced introduction to the topic, explaining the legal rules, rights and obligations applicable to activities in outer space and activities that precede operations in space. He analyses the interaction of these elements as well as how international organizations relate to the core tenets of space legislation.

Key features include:
- an accessible and engaging writing style
- a forward-looking approach to how technological developments will be addressed in law
- discussion of space law within the boundaries of technology, operations, economics and politics
- consideration of fundamental paradigm changes, such as the increasing commercialization and privatization of space activities.

This *Advanced Introduction* is ideal for advanced students looking for a clear and concise overview of space law. It also provides an entry point for academics and practitioners who need to understand the relationship between space and law.

Professor Dr. Frans G. von der Dunk was appointed Associate Professor for research purposes at the Faculty of Law and Administration, Lazarski University, Warsaw, Poland in February 2020, in addition to holding the Harvey and Susan Perlman Alumni / Othmer Chair of Space Law at the University of Nebraska College of Law, Lincoln, Nebraska, United States since January 2008.

He published the first comprehensive *Handbook of Space Law*, with a foreword by Apollo 9 astronaut Rusty Schweickart, in 2015. Since 2006, he has been the Series Editor of *Studies in Space Law*, published by Brill. In addition, he has written more than 200 articles and published papers, given more than 150 presentations at international meetings and was a visiting professor at over 30 universities and other academic institutions across the world. He was a signatory, together with various Nobel Prize winners, astronauts and cosmonauts, and other luminaries from the global science and entertainment community, of the 'Asteroid 100x Declaration', December 2014.

Von der Dunk is also the Founder and Director of Black Holes consultancy in space law and policy, based in Leiden, the Netherlands. As a consultant, Von der Dunk has advised numerous governments, international organizations and private sector entities on issues of space law and policy.

For more information see https://law.unl.edu/frans-von-der-dunk/ or http://www.black-holes.eu.